HALF OF ONE WORLD

BY FOSTER HAILEY

PACIFIC BATTLE LINE

HALF OF ONE WORLD

HALF OF ONE WORLD

FOSTER HAILEY

THE MACMILLAN COMPANY

NEW YORK 1950

First Printing

Printed in the United States of America

INTRODUCTION

I had just returned from a six-month postwar trip through the Far East for the New York *Times*. The day after I arrived home, I met an old friend on a suburban train enroute to the city. He expressed curiosity about my trip, about where I had been and what I had seen. I had hardly finished listing the eight countries I had visited, and certainly I had not been talking more than a minute or two, when it was obvious his interest was lost. As soon as he politely could do so, he changed the subject to Europe and to France, from whence his ancestors had come. His heart was in Paris, not in Nanking; his mental frontier was the river Rhine, not the river Yen.

My friend is, I fear, the typical American. For over three and one-half years the United States fought in the Pacific Basin the most terrible war in its history. Guadalcanal, Kunming, the Owen Stanley Range, Assam, Iwo Jima, Nagasaki were as often on America's tongue as Casablanca, Salerno, London, Paris, or Berlin. Yet once the war against Japan was won, the countries of Asia again were forgotten by most Americans, relegated to that cluttered attic of the mind where we store away the things we always plan to sort out and put in order some day, but seldom do. It is not surprising that this is so. All but 600,000 of the United States' 146,000,000 inhabitants have their ancestral roots in Europe, Africa, and the Middle East. The 600,000 Asiatics in the United States have hardly caused a ripple on our consciousness. This is as true of Seattle, San Francisco, and Los Angeles as it is of Chicago, St. Louis, New York, and Philadelphia.

To those few of us Americans who are interested in the Far East, this seems a tragic oversight which will change greatly the course of history. Because along the Asian littoral and on the Pacific islands, on one-tenth of the earth's surface, live over one-half of the world's peoples, proud conservators of a culture that was centuries old before there was ever a white man on the North American continent. And the one man of Western civilization in whom they have trust—or did have—is, or was, the American. At war's end, in 1945, the whole Far East looked to the people of the United States to help them solve their problems, to help them win their freedom from oppression, from want, from fear. We have let them down.

It is in an attempt to reverse that course, to arouse the interest of Americans in the Far East, that I have written this book. Not because I believe myself better informed than others, because I am not, but because I believe I do have some information about Asia and some ideas as to what should be done there that will be of interest and that will help to that better understanding I feel is so necessary if we are ever to have a peaceful world. Asia's problems are not of a kind that will solve themselves, or that time alone will solve. It will require the best intelligence we can muster for the task.

I visited in the fall of 1946 and the winter of 1946–1947, Japan, Korea, China, Indo-China, Malaya, Siam, Indonesia, and the Philippines. I have read since nearly all the current books about them. Before that, I had spent the first two years of World War II in the Pacific as a correspondent for the New York *Times*, having seen during that time the Solomons, New Hebrides, New Caledonia, the Fijis, the Tongan Islands, the Aleutians, New Zealand, Australia, and several hundreds of thousands of miles of Pacific Ocean from ship and plane.

The impressions and information I gathered during the war years, and on my trip two years ago, buttressed by information I have gathered since on Asia and conclusions based on those impressions and that information, provide the core of this book. Those are my qualifications.

This is not intended as a book of reference, as must be evident from the fact that it has neither footnotes nor a lengthy appendix. Where I thought a document would be of interest, I have inserted it in the text. I have not attempted a learned discussion of cultural patterns nor have I tried to explain the intricacies of internal political situations. I have used as few exotic and unpronounceable names as possible, and I shall not bore you with translations of Japanese, Korean, and Chinese names to English equivalents of "Little Plum Blossom," or similar nonsense. I have tried instead to make a complex and vast problem understandable to the average American.

FOSTER HAILEY

TABLE OF CONTENTS

HALF OF ONE WORLD

PART I. HALF OF ONE WORLD

CHAPTER 1. *The Struggle for Asia*

When the recorded Imperial Rescript of Emperor Hirohito accepting the terms of surrender outlined in the Potsdam Declaration were broadcast from Tokyo to the 5,000,000 Japanese troops and carpet baggers on the Asiatic mainland and in Oceania, a number of things began to happen in addition to the cessation of the war. The most important result of that broadcast of August 15, 1945, was the creation of a political vacuum among half the world's peoples. This presented to the West political problems fully as great and as pressing as were the economic ones.

Three years and eight months before, the military forces of the only Westernized nation of the Far East had challenged the white man for control of that great area and its people. In six months' time the Japanese had chased the Americans out of the Philippines, the British out of Hong Kong, Singapore, Malaya, and Burma, and the Dutch out of the Indies. Previously, they had made a deal with the Vichy French in Indo-China and won that rich country of 25,000,000 people without a fight. Not since Magellan and the other early explorers had discovered this land-poor, culturally rich, politically backward area of the world had the prestige of the West been so low in the East. What few white men remained were either interned or in hiding in the hills. The Government of the only halfway free country of Asia—China—had been driven back into the hinterlands where it could be easily contained.

The end of the war found the American Army back in the Philippines, in China in considerable force, and in control of the key islands over which Japan once had held mandates. The Russian Army was in Manchuria and North Korea. Britain was in Burma and on the way to Malaya. But the other two great colonial powers of Asia—France and the Netherlands—had neither the troops in the Pacific nor at home to move back in and reassert their sovereignty over Indo-China and the East Indies respectively. At Potsdam it had been decided that Southeast Asia was Britain's responsibility, so to her instead of to the United States was assigned the task of going into the Indies, into Siam, and into Indo-China to accept the surrender of Japanese troops and repatriate them. France had a few officials and a few native levies in her South Pacific islands, but not enough to make much of a show.

Siam was no great problem, because there was an extensive underground there which was just about ready to rise against the Japanese when the war ended. Indo-China and the Indies, however, were something quite different. Both were former colonies of European powers. In both there was a strong nationalist group that had composed what underground organization there was in both countries, since all the Dutch in the Indies had been interned and the French, in Indo-China, had been collaborating with the Japanese until within six months of the end of the war, when they too had been put in prison camps.

The British (aided in Indo-China by a Chinese division) moved into both Indonesia and Indo-China with an apparent intention to restore the territories to their colonial allies, the French and the Dutch. This attitude later was changed in Indonesia, and they helped work out there a formula that looked hopeful for peace until the Dutch became impatient and tried to impose their own solution by force. In Indo-China the British pulled out as soon as possible to let the French stew in their own juice, which the representatives of the Fourth Republic have been doing successfully.

China, Japan, and Korea (the south half of it) became, through the agreed-on division of responsibility, the headaches of the United States. Only in Japan have these been less than had been feared. The willing acquiescence of the Japanese to occupation, like children who felt a deep sense of guilt and were quite willing to atone by doing anything that teacher suggested, has been one of the more pleasant surprises of the postwar years. After struggling with the Soviet and with the Koreans in that unhappy country for three years, the United States dumped that problem in the lap of the United Nations. The Chinese situation proved incapable of solution by mediation, and the Nationalist Government there too weak a reed to be supported even by the pouring in of over $2,750,000,000. We settled that dilemma finally by withholding support from Chiang Kai-shek and letting the Chinese settle their quarrel themselves.

Although the situations in China, Indo-China, and Indonesia have many dissimilarities, they have one thing in common. The peoples of those lands are all strongly nationalistic. This is true of both sides in China. Chiang Kai-shek resented outside interference, even if he welcomed United States dollars, fully as bitterly as did the Chinese Communists. It was an attitude shared by most of the Chinese people. You could feel it in Peiping and Nanking and Shanghai even more than in Yenan. The feeling was similar to that of 1928, one American woman said, when, it will be remembered, American gunboats had to rescue Nanking's Americans and Europeans from their stronghold on Socony Hill. I had direct evidence of this myself in a Nanking café, where a table of Chinese next to that where I was sitting with Tillman Durdin, the New York *Times* chief correspondent in China, and his wife, became abusive both of their waiter and of us (in Chinese, which the Durdins understood) when we were given bone chopsticks and they only wood. The wives of United States Embassy officials were being jostled in crowds and Chinese everywhere were expectorating just shy of the shoes of the Americans they met on the streets.

Anti-Americanism is not so evident elsewhere. And it probably does not exist to any great extent outside of China. What does exist is a great disillusionment. Because of our expressed ideals, because of the record of the United States in the Philippines and the magnificent manner in which Americans fought and won the war in the Pacific and on the Continent, the people of Asia expected something much better from us than they have received. The United States went ahead with its promises in the Philippines—granting the Filipinos their independence on July 4, 1946—but in China we failed to drive a good bargain with the Nationalists which would have made the Chiang government palatable to most of the Chinese; and in Southeast Asia we played the part, in the first three postwar years, of a silent partner of the colonial powers.

United States' handling of the problem of Japan began to raise in 1948 outspoken questions as to our good intentions, or rather as to our intelligence. As each succeeding survey group to Japan lowered the total of reparations Japan would be required to pay to the countries she had ravished and enunciated even more forbidding programs for the rebuilding of Japanese industry, other Asiatics became more and more concerned about the possibility of a resurgent Japan that would dominate Asia economically in a few years, if not militarily. The Japanese constitution that was written by MacArthur's men renounced war as an instrument of Japanese policy and Japan was stripped of all her military arms and forces; but if the war-making potential remained in a strong steel industry, chemical plants, and so on, what is to prevent her, the other Asiatics argued, from some day, when Allied control has been withdrawn, of quickly rearming herself.

Unhappiest of all the "liberated" countries of Asia has been Korea. That small nation of 30,000,000, which Japan had held as a vassal since 1905, was caught between the United States and Soviet Russia and almost squeezed to death. By the time Secretary of State Marshall decided the impasse between Washington and Moscow was not going to be solved in the Joint Commission and had laid the problem before the United Nations, it was too late to achieve either a happy or peaceful solution. When the Red Army swept into the northern part of Korea and down to the 38th parallel in August and September of 1945, its leaders knew exactly what was wanted done. They took in with them Korean Communists who had been fighting against Japan in an underground in Manchuria, joined them with Korean Communists on the ground, and set up a People's Republic that proceeded forthwith to seize and divide the land and impose a totalitarian state in the Russian occupation zone. By the time the United Nations was seized of the problem, there was a strong government in operation in North Korea, organized down to the smallest village and with a militia, trained by the Red Army, of tens of thousands of men.

United States occupation forces, under Lieutenant General John R. Hodge, moved into South Korea armed only with good intentions. There was no well-thought-out plan for governance of the country. He was so intent on maintaining order that he even used the Japanese forces there to maintain it. Land reform was delayed for over two years, and the interim government that General Hodge set up (half of which was appointed by him) had neither the respect of the Americans nor the Koreans. The election of May, 1948, sponsored by the United Nations, was probably as honest an election as ever was held in Asia; but by that time Korea was irrevocably divided into two zones, and the Rhee government took office in August, 1948, under a terrific handicap. Without United States or United Nations protection it seemed destined for a short life. It will be many years before Korea possibly can live up to its name of "The Land of the Morning Calm." A cessation of the East-West conflict must precede peace in Korea.

Many Americans and Europeans have expressed surprise and concern at the extent and the growth of communism in Asia. The surprise should be that communism has not made greater progress than it has. Communism is the greatest revolutionary force in the world today. Until the Japanese attack it offered the only real hope for the nationalist leaders in China and Korea and Indo-China and Indonesia and the other colonial areas to achieve freedom in the span of their lives. The war and the fine promises that it brought to Asia of a New Deal after victory gave new hope to many of the nationalists that the whole world was on their side, that with peace would come freedom for them. Instead came confusion. The British freed India, Burma, and Ceylon and worked out in Malaya a fair compromise. But the United States gave uncritical support to

Chiang Kai-shek for many years, and what the Dutch and the French began doing again in Indo-China and in Indonesia as soon as they were strong enough appeared to the peoples of those countries to be the same old colonialism.

All of Asia's history, every instinct of its people, is against a communist state. The average Asiatic is more of an individualist than is the Englishman or the American. But if he is given no other choice, he must accept that. International communism, with its secret cells, its revolutionary doctrines, is the ideal underground. Stalin and Company didn't invent it. The system is as old as tyranny. Paul Revere, in the United States, belonged to a revolutionary "cell." So did George Washington and Benjamin Franklin and Thomas Jefferson. So did Simón Bolívar and San Martín in Latin America. It is the West which is forcing Asia toward communism.

There is still time to save Asia from domination by Moscow. Many of the nationalist leaders fear it. They would prefer to have an alternative. Ho Chi Minh, the leader of the Viet Namese, admits he was once a Comintern agent in Southeast Asia. Now, he says, "I am a Viet Namese." Communist influence in Indonesia was minor, despite Dutch propaganda to the contrary, until the Dutch began their police action there in July, 1947. It undoubtedly has been growing since. Communism flourishes only where there are great and evident evils to be overcome, as in China. It has made little progress since the war in India, or in the Philippines, or even in Japan. If Asia becomes communistic, as has eastern Europe, it will not be because of Moscow or because of Russian machinations. It will be because the West has not lived up to its wartime promises. Communism will win by default, not because the people of Asia thought it was the better way.

PART I. HALF OF ONE WORLD

CHAPTER 2. *One-Tenth the Land—One-Half the People*

Sister Pim Hoogenboezem, the Dutch nurse, led the American visitor to one of the wooden benches in the Dienst von Volk Gezonheid (Temporary Hospital for the People), in Batavia, Java, on which were stretched out, without covers or other protection from the flies and mosquitoes that swarmed under the low thatched roof in the steaming air, several hundred ill or injured Indonesians, Chinese, and other Asiatics who had been found in the streets of Batavia during the previous few days. On this bench lay a little Indonesian girl of perhaps four or five years. There was little flesh on the tiny bones under the brown skin. Sister Pim lifted the bandage that covered the left side of the little girl's face to disclose a ghastly hole that exposed her teeth and gums on that side.

"We had her almost cured two months ago and sent her home," said Sister Pim, as she replaced the bandage and patted the skinny little shoulder in an attempt to quiet the whimpers. "She was brought back to us two days ago as you see her now, worse than before. There apparently was just not enough food to go around. She is suffering from noma, which is a tissue disease brought on by starvation. When she is cured a second time, we must send her home again. We can do nothing else. We have room here only for the sick."

The nameless little girl on the hard wooden bench in the temporary hospital in a Batavia park epitomized the one great problem of Asia—too many people on too little land. It is a problem that is being added to each year. Despite death rates that are appalling by Western standards, the excess of births among the 900,000,000 in

China and India alone in normal times are believed to total at least 5,000,000 for each country each year. (Exact figures are simply not available anywhere in Asia.) It is not unreasonable to assume that among the 260,000,000 in the rest of the Far East there is an excess of births over deaths of at least 2,500,000 each year. World War II, the Chinese Civil War, the colonial wars in Indonesia and Indo-China, the communal rioting in India in 1947, and the inevitable camp follower of these violences—Famine—have alleviated the problem for the time being. But it is to accept a callousness beyond Christian comprehension that the world should deliberately let 40,000,000 persons die unnecessarily each seven years—as it is estimated that many have died in Asia since 1941: 5,000,000 in Indonesia during the war years and 20,000,000 of them in China in the first two postwar years to cite two generally accepted figures—without seeking some other solution.

Here is a problem to challenge the world's intelligence: over one-half the world's peoples living on one-tenth of the earth's surface (and not, by any means, the most productive one-tenth), living there in want, in misery, breeding like guinea pigs and dying by the millions each year from preventable diseases or in periodic famines. From one end of Asia to the other one walks always with misery by his side. It is not something he reads about only in his newspaper, which is the closest connection most Americans have with hunger and misery. The misery of Asia is always waiting the well-to-do outside his compound wall, in the gutter outside his European-style hotel, along the streets he walks or through which he rides in his automobile, his rickshaw, his pedacar, or *samlar*.

It is a misery about which little ever has been done or is being done in Asia today. In the West, and especially in the United States, there is the means, if it is properly distributed, to alleviate hunger and cure disease. Private and governmental agencies largely provide the ways. Few persons die of hunger or of preventable disease in the United States, in the United Kingdom, or in most countries of Europe. In the East there is neither the means nor the ways. Under present methods of cultivation the land does not provide enough food for the growing population. There is not the proper transportation system to distribute equitably even what is available. There has not been, except among the new revolutionary governments, apparently even the desire on the part of the ruling classes to seek a solution to this great problem of hunger. It is easier just to let nature take its course, which it does inexorably every few years.

This harsh judgment applies to the free governments of Asia as well as to the European colonial powers. Exploitation of the people was not something the white conquerors of the Far East imported. The kings, the emperors, the sultans of Japan, Korea, China, Indo-China, Indonesia, Malaya, and the rest had little more interest in the general welfare than did the colonial powers. The main interest of Asia's rulers for centuries has been profits and not people, the welfare of the few and not the welfare of the many, the maintenance of the status quo, whether it was war-lord rule or colonial rule, not the institution of a fair deal for all. The miseries of today are thus an accumulation of the centuries. But it is an accumulation which has reached such terrible dimensions that it can no longer be ignored by the West. The East now is at that point of which Edwin Markham spoke in the last stanza of his dramatic protest against exploitation of the many by the few, "The Man with the Hoe." Put a coolie's rags and a harvesting flail instead of a hoe in the hand of the work-bowed French peasant Millet painted, which inspired the San Francisco poet to his mighty outburst, and what Markham said in 1899 about the white workers of the world applies today to Asia's billion:

> O masters, lords and rulers in all lands,
> How will the future reckon with this Man?
> How answer his brute question in that hour
> When whirlwinds of rebellion shake all shores?
> How will it be with kingdoms and with kings—
> With those who shaped him to the thing he is—
> When this dumb Terror shall rise to judge the world,
> After the silence of the centuries?

The "dumb Terror" of Asia is at last awakening. Japan's aggression drove the white man out and showed the weakness both of the colonial powers and of Asia's own governments. It freed from jail or brought back from exile many of Asia's articulate leaders in the colonial areas. It gave them the opportunity to practice during the war years at least a modicum of national organization and self-government. As much as the other Asiatics came to hate the Japanese for their callousness and brutality, at least Japan had shown that an Asiatic country could, for a time at least, hold its own against the West. Most importantly, these new national leaders based their programs on the people, something the white man in Asia has never done. Through the radio networks that had been set up by the Japanese to spread their false doctrine of "Asia for the Asiatics," which the other peoples of Asia finally learned to understand should have been stated as "Asia for the Japanese," they have reached through the ear many of the 90 to 95 per cent of Asia's billion who could not be reached through the printed page. Their programs all were essentially the simple four points set by President Ho Chi Minh of Viet Nam, the leader of the independence movement in Indo-China: food for the people; education of the people; political and religious freedom for the people; peaceful relations with other countries. It might be summarized as a government, of, by, and for the people.

Which of the basic points of the nationalist programs have the most appeal, only a poll of the people could determine. It has always been the belief of cynical governments that the first point is the determining factor in human behavior. Food is important; a hungry man makes a poor citizen. But if we are to believe that that characteristic which most distinguishes man from animal is his spirit, or soul, then another yardstick must be applied. The appeal also must be to that inner self and not to his stomach alone. The fortitude with which the people of the nationalist movements have pursued their goal, as I have seen it, is proof enough for me that the man of Asia is no different from the man of the other continents; he will make any sacrifice to call his soul his own.

Every ruler of Asia for centuries, and especially the colonial powers of the last three hundred years, have treated the Asiatic in large part as though he were an ox, without the same feeling as men of lighter skin. Until these new nationalist leaders came along to base in the people their campaigns for freedom, little attempt had been made to treat the great masses as human beings. They were statistics in a table, of no more importance than, or even as much as, the figures on imports, exports, and profits. This was not as individuals, of course. I do not doubt the sincerity of the affection white individuals had for brown, yellow, or black-skinned Asiatics as individuals. But not in the mass. Never in the mass. That is in the record. It cannot be erased.

It was probably this difference in color that encouraged the white man (or "European," as most white people are called in Asia) to the conquests which are only now, at long last, being thrown off by Asia, and which, eventually, will be broken in Africa, too, I believe. Among ourselves we vehemently deny any essential differences. Psychologically, Hitler's trumpeting of his "master race" theories was one of his great errors. It set even his own allies, the Italians, against him and his Germans. But we whites, as a race, have tended to view all those of other skin pigmentation as inferior to us. We don't speak of Englishmen as natives of England, or Frenchmen as natives of France, or Dutchmen as natives of the Netherlands. But we and they speak of the natives of Malaya, the natives of Indo-China, and the natives of Indonesia—with the usual derogatory inflection, of course. In two wars the fighting men of the Allied nations have called the Germans "Jerry" or "Fritz." Worse names, too, of course, but mostly those. Yet the common appellation for the Japanese among the Americans in the Pacific was "those yellow bastards," with the accent on the adjective.

Apparently because he was the first to make full use of the machine, especially in the waging of war, the white man has considered himself superior to the men of other color. Biologically there seems some basis for this since the white strain always predominates in mixtures of blood. In science, too, the white races have far outstripped the colored. But in art, and especially in the art of living—which should be considered the apex of man's development—the East is far ahead of the West. The East had a well developed culture while the West still was making mud pies. Perhaps when most of us have been atomized by atomic bombs—the epitome of our scientific progress—and our great machine-made cities reduced to rubble, the art of Asia will be found to be more enduring than the science of the West.

I like, in this connection, the story told by Hadji Agoes Salim, the elder, at sixty-five, of Indonesian nationalism, as we sweated out the sixteen-hour-long train ride from Batavia to Jogjakarta, on Java, one steamy January day in 1947. We had been talking about the "White Australia" policy—which excludes all men of color as permanent residents of the "down under" continent—and the customary arrogant assumption of superiority of the white man. Old Hadji, his eyes twinkling and his sparse beard bobbing as he talked, said that the Indonesians had their own version of the creation of man. God, he said, had to do some experimenting when he first molded the clay of the riverbank in his own image and breathed into it the breath of life. His first effort he left in the drying oven too long and it turned black. He made another little figure but, overcautious now, did not leave it in the oven long enough and it emerged half-baked and colorless. These two failures had given God the right formula, so on the third try he achieved the effect he had been seeking, a man with a skin of golden brown. "Ah," said God, "that is just right."

Later, back in the States, I heard the white version. An acquaintance who had spent many years in Indonesia with an American oil firm was trying to explain to a group of us why he thought the Dutch were right in asserting their "sovereignty" in Indonesia after the war. The Dutch had learned, he said, that they could never really educate the Indonesians. To the age of seven years, the white boy and the brown boy showed about the same rate of progress in their studies. Then the white boy began to forge ahead.

The brown could never catch up. The white boy was better able to assimiliate what, I wonder: knowledge of how best to handle a machine gun or a tank or a fighter plane?

This question of color is an important part of the problem of East-West relations. Most Europeans in Asia pooh-pooh it and don't like to talk about it. But the articulate Asiatics will tell you that either consciously or subconsciously all the people of Asia resent it. They resent the clubs whose main rooms are barred to them. They resent the "Europeans only" signs just as bitterly as the Negroes in the United States resent the Jim Crow signs in our South. How much a part this is of the present hatred and distrust of the white man in Asia I do not know. But I would think it was a very important part. Until we learn to accept them as equals, we shall have hard going.

This racial superiority idea is what has led the white man, I believe, to use Asia only for his own ends. And there can be little question that that is what he has done. Three hundred years after the European trading companies first firmly established themselves in the Far East, that continent and its people are in far worse condition than they were when the white man first sailed in.

The Asia the white man found was not the most hospitable of the continents, although there are sections of it that have a good climate. It was not, though, the fertile, virgin land that was North America. It is what Professor Glenn Thomas Trewartha, of the University of Wisconsin, one of the world's leading geographers, calls the "monsoon realm," subject to steady winds which blow off the ocean in the summer, bringing downpours of rain, then reverse and bring dust and cold off the inner reaches of the continent in winter.

The drenching rains of summer and the high temperatures that prevail everywhere except in North China, Manchuria, Korea, and Japan's northern island of Hokkaido, and the cold winds of the dry winters have blown away and leached away the soluble mineral plant foods from the soil, leaving residual soils that are of low fertility and of little depth, especially on the uplands. The denuding of the hills of their tree growth in China accelerated this erosion by wind and water. It tended to crowd more and more of Asia's populations in the river valleys—along the route of the Yangtze, the Hwang (Yellow River) and the Hung Shu in China, the Irrawaddy in Burma, the Mehong and Red rivers in French Indo-China, and the Ganges and the Brahmaputra in India.

Another reason for this concentration along the rivers was that they are still today, as they always have been, the main arteries of communication. Whereas Western man has freed himself of the rivers as principal transportation media by means of his railways, his hard roads, and his motor-driven vehicles, the Asiatic still largely travels by river boat, oxcart, or on his own two strong legs. Any visitor to the Fiji Islands, in the South Pacific, must be struck by the magnificent leg development of these people. Since ages eternal—as the Japanese expresses his national life—the Fijians have depended on shank's mare to take them from here to there, and it shows in the size and contour of their calf and their thigh muscles.

In 1937, when Japan began its "China Incident," as it always called its war there, China had only 59,886 miles of roads across its vast distances, of which only 11,398 miles were paved, and only 8,131 miles of railways to serve its 2,903,475 square miles of area. Contrast this with the United States, whose 2,973,776 square miles of area are only slightly greater than that of China. The United States, in 1937, had 3,009,066 miles of roads, of which 693,559 were hard-surfaced, and 254,347 miles of railway trackage. The same contrast is valid for the rest of Asia, with the exception of Japan. The spread is even greater today. Since 1937 the years have seen an increase in United States road mileage and railway trackage but an enormous deterioration of Asia's railways and roadways through war damage and neglect.

The concentration of population in the river valleys has resulted in an overcrowding of the land that is almost beyond comprehension. Even were Asia's billions evenly distributed over the whole areas of Japan, Korea, China, India, and the other countries, the density per square mile would be great enough. China's population density per square mile, calculated on that basis, is 231, India's, 246; Japan's, 375; Java's, 950, and Malaya's, 95. That of the United States is 44.2 persons per square mile. When the more populous areas of Asia are considered, the contrast becomes staggering. Take, for instance, the population of the Kowloon Peninsula, opposite Hong Kong. There 125,055 persons are crowded into each square mile. Those who slept three and four to a room in Washington during the war years probably thought that was the most crowded area on earth. But at Washington's peak the population density was only 10,870 to the square mile, and even New York's crowded five boroughs have only an average of 26,000 persons to each square mile of apartment house and pavement.

Manhattan's lower East Side and Harlem areas are bad enough, as is London's crowded East End along the Thames River docks, Washington's Negro areas, and Chicago's near South Side. But walk or drive through Singapore's poorer areas, through Shanghai's Chapei district, through some of the kampongs in Batavia, through Calcutta's slum areas, and a new measuring rod for misery will be found.

One evening during the summer of 1947 I was returning to midtown by taxi after dinner at the Claremont Inn on upper Riverside Drive with some of the Indonesian Republicans who were in New York presenting their case to the Security Council of the United Nations. I told the driver to take us through Harlem. The night had softened some of the harsh outlines of the area and concealed the garbage and rubbish-strewn vacant lots, but it still did not look like Park Avenue to my eyes. I explained that Harlem was New York's worst slum area. "Slums," said my Indonesian friends. "Are these blocks your worst slums?" Remembering Shanghai and Singapore and Batavia and Bangkok and Nanking, a second look also changed my viewpoint. At least the buildings are roofed against the rain. If any of the people we saw along the sidewalks became ill, an ambulance was on call and hospitalization waiting only a few blocks away. There were no beggars along the sidewalk peddling their infirmities and open sores. There was no one dying in the gutters of malnutrition. Dysentery, smallpox, and other communicable diseases were not endemic in the area through which we were riding. All those facets of human misery are a commonplace in Asia.

These great physical differences between the United States, prewar Europe, and most of Asia provide problems that are foreign to us and that require more drastic remedies than we are accustomed to consider. The Eastern religions, that touch every small issue of life, from birth to death, are so far from the Christian pattern that it is easy to indulge in the sophistry that there never can be a meeting of minds or ideas between East and West. It is the excuse given by those white men who would like to return to the old ways of political and economic exploitation for resistance to the growth of nationalism in Asia.

Political and economic problems cannot be separated in Asia any more than they can in Europe. We found that out in the operation of the European Recovery Program. Yet the colonial powers in Asia have insisted that the old political system should be retained until the "native" populations have achieved economic stability and political maturity. Consciously and openly, or subconsciously, they have been counting on this Asiatic backwardness and the stagnation of the thinking of the great masses of people there to enable them to do this. As one colonial official in Indonesia was reported to me to have told a staff conference during the nonshooting period of negotiation with the Republic of Indonesia, "If we play our cards right, we can stay here another hundred years."

At a luncheon conference with a British official in New York shortly after the end of the war and before the British Government's decision to grant independence to India and permit partition of the Moslem and Hindu states, Max Lerner put the question clearly, "What you are asking the Indians," he asked, "is to fight their civil war first before embarking on their war of independence, isn't it?" Fortunately for Britain, and for India, a war of independence was not made necessary. Britain granted India her right to decide her own destiny. Although it involved partition and bloody communal rioting in the great migrations that followed after August 15, 1947, there is growing hope both in the Indian Union and in Pakistan that reunion may some day be achieved. The Moslems, especially, are seeing the disadvantages they brought on themselves by insisting on a division on religious grounds alone. It is economic and political forces that are drawing them together again.

The old standards cannot be applied to Asia today. A new spirit walks the countries of the Far East and it will not be denied. The white man would be well advised to go with the tide. If he attempts to hold it back, he will be no more successful than was King Canute. It will overwhelm him and it might lead to events that are too horrible to contemplate, a contest of race and of color. The Asiatic phases of World War II made a drastic change in the picture of the world.

PART II. JAPAN AND KOREA

CHAPTER I. *Fujisan*

The sun had just disappeared behind the mountains as the Army Transport Command's C-54 passenger plane made its landfall south of Tokyo and started its glide toward Haneda Airfield, midway between the Japanese capital and Yokohama. It had taken off four hours before in the hot glare of midafternoon from Iwo Jima. There everything was clearly etched under the burning sun. Now, in the afterglow and the cool air at 7,000 feet, the world had a softer outline. The small islands off the Honshu coast looked like something out of a Japanese painting. The twelve passengers in the plane—two civilians and ten Army men—crowded the windows on the port side. Above the broken cloud layer at 6,000 feet rose the landmark of a country—the white-crested peak of Fujisan, the extinct volcanic cone that dominates the Kanto Plain. Clearcut among shadows, it looked exactly as they all had expected it to look.

Fuji is a symbol of conquered, occupied Japan—a shell of a mountain; a shell of a country. Fuji's 12,389-foot symmetrical sides dominate the main coastal plain of Japan's main island. In a like manner, the small people who look to it with pride and reverence once hoped to dominate the world; perhaps they still do. But Japan and the Japanese, like Fuji, are today burned out. Eighty-one of Japan's principal cities were, in various degrees, bombed and burned. More than 5,000,000 of her young men have died since 1937 in Manchuria, in China, in Southeast Asia, in the Philippines, on Guadalcanal, New Guinea, Iwo Jima, and other of the Pacific islands. Over 250,000 more of her people died violently at home during the bombings; almost 100,000 of them in two split seconds in Hiroshima and Nagasaki under the paralyzing radioactive heat of the atomic bomb. Several millions more were wounded or became ill because of war rigors. Of all the buildings in Japan, 17 per cent, or almost 2,500,000, were destroyed and 15 per cent of her homes (2,000,000). Her colonial empire has been taken from her. Korea has been "liberated" (about which more will be said later). Manchuria, Formosa, and the Pescadores have been returned to China. The Kurile Islands and the lower half of Karafuto, or Sakhalin, were taken by Russia under the terms of the Yalta Agreement. We have possession of the former mandates of the Carolines, Marshalls, and Marianas and of Okinawa and other of the Ryukyus. She faces at least some measure of foreign control for an indeterminate future.

What remains of the Japanese Empire, that for a time in the early months of the war was composed of Korea, Manchuria, a quarter of China, Indo-China, Burma, most of the Netherlands East Indies, and almost a billion people, are the four main islands of Honshu, Hokkaido, Shikoku, and Kyushu, and a few outlying small islands. Only her own nationals—an estimated 77,000,000—remain as subjects of the emperor.

What fifty-two years of aggression finally has cost Papa-san and Mama-san and all the little Japanese was partially evident before the wheels of the Army transport plane touched the sacred soil that Tojo and Yamamoto had promised would never be defiled by a conqueror's boot. For miles, between Yokohama and Tokyo, stretched a forest of factory chimneys. But no factories. The chimneys were all that remained. In contrast to an evening approach to a comparable city in the United States, there were few lights showing, either along the streets or in the houses. The air was clear for there was no factory smoke to obscure the view. Although it was October, and the air was chilly, there was little smoke coming from any residence chimneys either.

An Army weapons carrier loaded the baggage, to take it into the ATC terminal in Tokyo. The passengers, however, were directed to a wheezing Japanese bus that certainly had seen better days. At the wheel was what apparently was a former Japanese soldier. He was still dressed in his uniform—the poorly fitting jacket, baggy pants, wrap leggings, and small, peaked cloth cap. Except for the lack of insignia, he looked just like the ones the Marines had killed on Guadalcanal four years before.

The bus was like everything else Japanese. It was a poor imitation of an American bus. It was about to fall to pieces. The seats were built for the five-foot Japanese. Its American passengers had to curl their long legs around their hand luggage or extend them into the narrow aisle. When the sullen little driver saw that all his passengers were aboard, he gingerly swung shut the door and started the bumpy six-mile journey into Tokyo.

It was like a ride through a Negro suburb of many southern cities in the United States. The roads were never very good in the first place. Now the Japanese driver had to weave through an uneven pattern of holes. There were no street lights. In the open-front, wooden houses that lined either side of the street flush with the sidewalks, there seldom was more than one dim bulb burning. In that poor light, families of eight and ten persons were sitting around tables eating or working. Every few houses there was a small machine shop, sometimes with a small forge glowing. These—both the homes and the small machine shops—were the remnants of the so-called "shadow factories" to which the war plants sent out small piecework during Japan's days of conquest. This dispersal of industry through every city area was one of the reasons why it was decided to use against Japan the area-bombing tactics in which our planes seldom took part over Europe. Over Europe, it was a British night-bombing technique.

By some miracle the Japanese driver pulled up in the alley alongside the ATC terminal without having run down any of the almost countless bicyclists whom the bus had careened past in its left-hand-side-of-the-street journey through the city. (Changing over to right-hand driving was one major reform General MacArthur did not attempt.) The bicyclists, who had been only dimly seen in the flickering lights of the bus, seemed oblivious to their danger. Many of them were riding along with only one hand on the handlebars. The other hand was used to support a youngster or a package on the rack behind the seat.

The brightly lighted terminal and the adjoining modern buildings, including the Dai Aichi Building, which was selected as occupation headquarters, were in brilliant contrast to the one-story shacks along most of the route. The modern part of Tokyo, which is concentrated in the area east of the Imperial Palace, together with most of the modern buildings along the nameless street that runs in front of the palace—called "Imperial Hotel Street" by most of the Americans because the earthquake-proof hotel Frank Lloyd Wright designed faces on it—were little hurt by the bombing.

That part of the city was not a prime military objective, since it contained only office buildings and hotels. And it also was fireproof and largely shockproof. It was protected also by its proximity to the Imperial Palace which, for reasons that escaped many Americans who knew that the Japanese probably would show no such compunction toward the White House if they had a like opportunity, was marked off limits for the B-29's. An occasional "near miss" did fall in the area, even a few bombs on buildings in the many-acred Imperial Palace grounds. But traveling through only that area, the visitor saw few signs of war or of bombings. There was even little camouflage. The six-story Radio Tokyo building, which housed most of the Japanese propaganda agencies, was one of the few exceptions. It was streaked with the favored Japanese dark-brown and green camouflage pattern.

Elsewhere through the city, outside the factory areas, the evidences of the great fire raids made by the B-29's is spotty. The American Embassy, where General MacArthur lived with his wife, Jean, and their small son, was untouched, as were several of the other embassies. Many of the homes of the wealthier Japanese, set in small parks, also were not damaged. Most of the wooden houses of Tokyo, where Papa-san and Mama-san lived, however, were burned to heaps of ashes. Those Japanese who remained in the city

—before war's end almost half the population had been killed, had been wounded, or had left the city—crowded in with relatives or salvaged enough tin and boards to build small shacks along the streets and take up life again there as best they could.

Unlike most of the rest of Asia a year after war's end, however, Tokyo and the other cities of Japan were tidy and their people were orderly. The salvagable materials from the burned-out buildings and factories were either cleaned and piled in neat rows or were being used for reconstruction. Factory sites had been cleared of ashes and rubble and vegetable gardens planted among the lonely chimneys. Electric facilities had been restored, where it was possible, and there was little necessity for a householder to keep candles at hand in every room in anticipation of an electric failure halfway through dinner. Trains again were running on schedule, pulling into shattered terminals such as the main station in Tokyo almost exactly to the timetable.

How much of this orderliness was due to occupation policy and to thoroughness in execution and how much to the inherent qualities of the Japanese people it is impossible to say. As good a guess as any probably would be 50 per cent credit to each. The occupation of Japan by Allied troops—largely American—was well conceived and has been well carried out. Under MacArthur's direction essential services were restored much more quickly and much more efficiently than other Oriental peoples were able to restore their electric light, water, and power facilities. And this despite the fact that Japan was the more seriously battered of all Asiatic countries. For one thing, in order to make the occupation successful the Allies had to restore order in Japan. To secure power for the factories that were under Allied control, power facilities had to be restored for all Japan. To provide transportation for Allied troops, railway lines had to be repaired over which trains for the Japanese also could move. A resurfaced highway was available for Japanese transport just as it was for military vehicles.

But occupation policy is not the complete story. The Japanese himself must be given some credit. Although of the Orient, he is not entirely Oriental. It has never been Japanese custom to sit and contemplate the navel when there was work to be done. As one United States official in Japan expressed it one day, in discussing the contrast between the chaos in China—where he had long served—and the orderliness in Japan: "The Chinese is more intelligent, but the Japanese is more energetic." A similar comparison could be made between the Japanese and almost every other Oriental.

Since the Meiji Restoration of 1868, which marks the beginning of the rise of modern Japan, the Japanese has looked to the East, to the United States, for his pattern of living, instead of West to the Orient. Like all imitations of an original, the Japanese way has not reached the standard of the Western countries, especially in industrialization. This was amply proven during the war. Most of his war weapons were second-rate. They were good, but not good enough. The Japanese reached his peak on December 7, 1941. Then he started downhill. It was the failure of many military leaders—which was true especially among the United States admirals in Washington—correctly to evaluate this factor that led to the "surrender" to the Soviet at Yalta by President Roosevelt and Prime Minister Churchill, who had been advised that the aid of the Red armies was necessary to defeat Japan. By 1945 the United States was sufficiently powerful to do the job alone. Japan was ready to fall down. All she needed was a final push. Probably not even the atom bomb was needed, although the Hiroshima and Nagasaki drops undoubtedly helped the Japanese leaders make up their minds. Emperor Hirohito was asking peace terms three months before that sunny August morning when the first A-bomb dropped out of the belly of a B-29 over the unsuspecting city of Hiroshima.

The Japanese surrender, and the subsequent occupation, gave the Japanese a boon they otherwise would not have had. It is the forced application to Japanese industry, to the Japanese Government, to Japanese living, of Western techniques. Representatives of Supreme Commander Allied Powers, or SCAP, as it is always referred to in Japan, sit in as advisors on practically every Japanese operation, industrial, educational, or political. The illusion is maintained that the Japanese are being allowed to run all their own affairs, that MacArthur and his men are in Japan only to see that order is maintained. It doesn't fool anyone, especially the Japanese. They know who is boss. But the more intelligent Japanese welcome this intrusion. In the ruins of their cities, the destruction of their fleets, they have had ample evidence that they are not yet the equal of the West. Why shouldn't they welcome the application of American industrial techniques to their textile factories, to their mining operations, to their power setups, to their railways, to all their transportation methods? Their leaders remember that on Adak, in the Aleutians, a few Army engineers built in twelve days a better airfield than Japanese engineers were able to build on Kiska in a year. They have seen and admired United States bulldozers and levelers, dredgers, pile drivers and other construction equipment doing in hours what their machines would require days to do.

Battered as were Japan's cities and her factories, three and one-half years after her defeat, she was in better financial and physical shape than most other areas. Despite large subsidies to producers of coal, fertilizers, steel, and other basic industrial items, the Japanese Government was maintaining a near balance of the budget, manufacturing was near the break-even point despite considerable increase in labor costs as compared to prewar, and the decision to allow trade between Japan and sterling areas such as Hong Kong, Singapore, Malaya, and India promised a big upturn in export trade.

Much of Japan's economic health was due, of course, to United States assistance. How great this should be was left to the determination of General MacArthur. He was limited only by the vague phrase that it should be an amount necessary to "prevent disease and unrest." In 1947 the value of imports of food and raw materials, principally petroleum and cotton for Japan's textile mills, amounted to $526,130,000, and in 1948 to approximately $650,000,000. These large sums were for Japanese aid alone. To them must be added the costs of maintenance of our occupation army of 80,-000 to 100,000 men and the civilian components of SCAP, all of which were being paid for by the United States with scant hope of repayment from Japan. Against this total inflow of goods and services of a total value of more than $1,000,000,000 a year, Japan exported in 1947 goods of a value of $173,568,000, mostly textiles, and in 1948, of a value of $250,000,000. Favorable trade balances were maintained only with Asiatic countries.

This is not a bright record, but it was so much better than most other Asiatic countries that it was raising justifiable fears for the future in all of them. Before the triumph of the Communists in China, there was considerable talk among the Nationalists in Nanking of a tariff barrier against Japanese goods. The Chinese could see Japan again becoming the economically dominant country of Asia, which, in a peaceful world, would be almost as bad, from the Chinese viewpoint, as a militarily dominant Japan. This fear also was expressed by Philippine spokesmen, where hatred of Japan was probably more deeply imbedded even than in China. The late President Roxas refused to allow Japanese textiles to be put on sale in Manila because of the justifiable fear that the Filipinos would destroy them.

The changing United States attitude up through early 1949 toward the question of reparations from Japan, toward the rebuilding of capital goods industries such as steel, and the growing feeling among some Government officials and also among the American people that our recent enemy should be rebuilt and even rearmed as a bastion against communism gave reasonable ground for these fears among the people of Asia who had suffered so much, so recently, from Japanese aggression.

Each successive American commission to study Japan reduced the reparations total and raised the level of industrial production she was to be allowed to reach. All protested only that they were but recommending for Japan that level of production which would make her self-sufficient and thus lift a load from the shoulders of the American taxpayer, but it provided a frightening prospect for the other people of Asia and Oceania. The Overseas Consultants, Inc., whose report was made public by the Army in the spring of 1948, recommended, for instance, that Japan be allowed a steel-ingot production of 7,000,000 tons annually, which is almost the total Japan produced yearly during the war. The same group recommended that the synthetic oil plants, which provided the gasoline for the kamikaze planes that did such terrible damage to the United States fleets off Okinawa during the closing phases of the war, be taken off the reparations list since they could be converted to fertilizer manufacture. They could also be reconverted, the other Asiatics pointed out.

A committee headed by Percy H. Johnston, former New York banker, whose other members were Paul G. Hoffman, Robert F. Loree, and Sidney H. Scheuer, making a later survey in 1948, went even beyond the report of the Overseas Consultants. They marked off the reparations list many machine-tool factories, which, of all Japanese plants, are most vitally needed in other areas of Asia, if those former sufferers from Japanese aggression are to be enabled to build up industries that will make them less dependent on Japanese goods. They urged that Japan be allowed to increase "substantially" the merchant fleet that had been decided previously she was to have (about 20 per cent of prewar tonnage), that the limit of size be lifted, and that she be allowed to retain a greater part of her shipbuilding plant and even be allowed to accept foreign orders to keep it busy. As an alternative, the committee suggested bare-boat charter by Japan of vessels needed to reestablish foreign trade. Which would seem to be a preferable alternative, since there are hundreds of thousands of tons of American wartime shipping tied up in reserve fleets. If Japan is to be allowed a merchant navy again, to cut down the shipping costs—largely American—of her foreign trade, many observers believe it would be far safer to give her the ships than to permit her to have the shipyards, which, like the synthetic oil plants, could be easily and quickly converted to war uses.

The Johnston committee estimated that for Japan to maintain a standard of living comparable to prewar she will need a yearly export trade of $1,575,000,000 (at current prices), an increase of eight to nine times the 1948 total. This estimate envisions normal population growth and a fairly stable Far East, neither of which is certain. It also, presumably, envisions better land utilization and food production within the country, both of which, American experts believe, is possible.

The main question of Japanese rehabilitation would seem to be one of timing. Japan has been much better off since the end of the war, both foodwise and industrywise, than any other part of Asia except the Philippines. There has been no starvation in Japan and even very little unemployment, despite the 5,000,000 that had been repatriated from other countries through 1948. If the United States rebuilds Japan too rapidly, there is no question that she will again become economically dominant in Asia. It is not our fault, of course, that China has been so wracked by civil war. But the United States had done little, three and one-half years after the end of the war, to help settle the colonial problem in Southeast Asia, which had to precede any rehabilitation in Indonesia and Indo-China. It had done even less to rehabilitate South Korea industrially. By concentrating on Japan it had raised suspicions both of American intentions and of American sanity among other Asiatics.

It is true that Japan renounced war in its new Constitution of 1946 and its army, navy, and air force had been destroyed or disbanded. But all Asia knew, as well as did the Japanese, that the constitution was written in MacArthur's headquarters, not by the Japanese themselves. And they asked the reasonable question of how the United States proposed to see that the constitution remained unaltered and Japan remained unarmed once a peace treaty was negotiated and she was freed of United States control.

Brigadier General Carlos P. Romulo, Philippine ambassador to the United Nations, expressed what are undoubtedly the sentiments of most of free Asia's leaders when, in commenting on the Overseas Consultants recommendations, he said:

If the bulk of Japan's industrial machinery is preserved intact, there would be nothing to prevent her (once occupation forces are withdrawn) from blundering again into the vicious cycle of expansion and exploitation, aggression and war. Her neighbors, denied the means to strengthen themselves, will find it next to impossible to contain her resurgent power or curb her aggressive designs. . . . Japan can be restored as an industrial and military power only at the cost of alienating the rest of the Far East from the Allied cause. A dubious recruit would be gained at the cost of undermining the moral foundation of the alliance that proved stronger than three years of defeat and ultimately vanquished the common foe.

Unlike Fujisan (or Fujiyama, as most Americans know it), which volcanologists say will forever remain a shell, the Japanese State gives every indication of being in a decade, or less, the economic leader of the Orient, a thriving, industrialized nation that will have such a head start on every other country of Asia that it is doubtful her position can be successfully challenged. The peoples of the rest of Asia may well be asking, "Who won the war?"

PART II. JAPAN AND KOREA

CHAPTER 2. *Tojo and Papa-san*

In Row 1, Seat 1, of the middle section of the prisoners' dock in the War Crimes courtroom in the former War Ministry Building on a hill behind the Imperial Palace in Tokyo sat former Premier-General Hideki Tojo, a brown, bald-headed, bespectacled little man in the insignia-stripped uniform of the former Japanese Army. He was just over five feet tall and weighed about 110 pounds.

Tojo was the No. 1 war criminal of Japan. There were twenty-five others in the dock, but the wartime leader of Japan was the person all visitors first looked for when they entered the chilly, austere room where a way of life—the Japanese way—was on trial before a tribunal of representatives of eleven nations, and the world.

His name for years was the symbol of warring Japan. The Japanese soldier was not given the descriptive nickname, which showed some respect, that was given the German and the Italian by Americans. Most of the Americans who fought him called the Japanese "Tojo," or worse. On Guadalcanal in 1942 the Marines and sailors called the period between 11:00 A.M. and 2:00 P.M.—which was when the enemy bombers from Rabaul customarily arrived for their daylight attacks—"Tojo Time." His name meant barbarity. His name meant to the Americans who fought the Japanese everything they hated and which they were fighting.

Others of the twenty-six on trial sometimes looked around the courtroom. Occasionally the head of one or more would droop as he nodded sleepily through the monotonous sessions, with their repetitious translations in several tongues of everything that was said. Not Tojo. He sat straight in his chair, looking across prosecution and defense counsel to the judges and the big windows behind them through which could be seen the roofs of the Imperial Palace and downtown Tokyo.

Immediately after the war Tojo was a hated name even among the Japanese. He had committed the unpardonable sin of losing a war that he had begun, of leading a nation to disaster. They argued that he represented something they had put behind them, which was that they were a race that was born to rule the world. As a representative of the old order he had even failed in the final act of a defeated samurai: his attempt at suicide was unsuccessful.

There was a change in the Japanese attitude toward Tojo as the trial dragged wearily along, with little publication of the case that was made against him and his codefendants. When Tojo made his arrogant and defiant defense of his actions, he became almost a hero again for a few days. And when he died in stoical fashion on the gallows, after first writing a poem, he was, perhaps, assuring himself of at least a measure of the respect from the average Japanese that he had seemed to lose.

The trial of the Japanese war criminals became almost a farce at the end, which was not relieved greatly by the stern verdicts that were handed down—death for Tojo and long prison terms for most of the others. If he lives long enough, General MacArthur may be able to say, "I told you my way was better," to those who disapproved of his plan to try the top Japanese military men in courts-martial on the charge of waging illegal and brutal war, as he did try Yamashita in Manila for the excesses of Japanese soldiers in the Philippines.

What Papa-san—the average Japanese—thinks of all the American actions, including the war crimes trials and the discredited Japanese leaders, would require a crystal ball to determine. Papa-san wears as imperturbable a mask as did Tojo. Or so it seems to most Americans. At home he may laugh and cry, show sorrow or anger or affection or disdain or disbelief. In public he does not. Oh, he may show his teeth occasionally in what passes for a smile. He will hiss politely and agree to almost anything that is said to him. But it would be a very rash person indeed who would dare to say what were Papa-san's thoughts.

For instance, there is Jo-jo, the little Japanese who was assigned by SCAP to drive the New York *Times*'s beaten-up old Packard convertible that a friendly United States Navy captain hauled out to Tokyo from Honolulu shortly after the surrender for the use of the *Times* staff. Months later neither Lindsay Parrott, chief of the *Times* Bureau in Tokyo, nor his wife Marian, nor anyone else knew much about Jo-jo. All that was known—and this was from his record—was that he lived in Yokohama, some twenty miles away, that he had a wife and five children, that he formerly drove a taxicab, and that he was about the same size as Tojo but twenty or thirty years younger and with a full head of straight black hair. He appeared each morning, drove the car where he was ordered to drive it, and disappeared each evening.

Jo-jo probably understood more English than he pretended. You never had to tell him twice where you wanted to go. He never spoke any English, however, or gave vocal evidence that he knew any. He responded to orders merely by a nod or by starting the car in the right direction. You never had to look for Jo-jo when you came out of a building where he had driven you. He always saw you first and had the car started and ready to pick you up before you were conscious of the necessity.

Warmhearted Marian Parrott, who was accustomed to belabor with some Japanese phrases she had learned for that purpose any driver she saw mistreating his horse, said she had tried to learn something of Jo-jo's home life and the condition of his family in the hope she might be able to furnish help if it was needed, but she had been unsuccessful. All she knew about Jo-jo or her other servants was that they were faithful, that they showed up at the appointed hours each day and never complained about extra duties.

It was the same with the other Japanese with but few exceptions. Two American correspondents were invited one morning to attend a class in industrial management at Meiji University, in Tokyo. After short talks, which the professor translated, they were asked questions by the students. And they in turn asked questions of the students. There was some laughter when one of the women students said she had no plans after graduation except to get married. Most of the time the translated questions and answers evoked no emotion whatever, whether they were about democracy, the atom bomb, or the place of women in modern Japan. One girl rose to ask one of the correspondents if he believed the United States was justified in dropping the atom bomb on Hiroshima. All her family had been killed by it, she said. A question as to the life of American movie actresses was put with a no less serious expression. The questions, of course, showed a wide range of thought. But they all were asked in the same monotone. The correspondents were not even conscious of being stared at when they entered the room, as they would have been stared at had they entered any comparable lecture hall in a Western university. How long before a people can be taught to be curious about life and other people after centuries of strict obedience to professor, father, emperor, and a dead past?

Certainly it can hardly be done in five years—which is the limit General MacArthur is said to believe military occupation should be imposed—and it may not be possible to accomplish any basic changes in Japanese character short of two or three generations. However, if the environment can be changed sufficiently, a start can be made. It is doubtful whether the necessity of doing that is not being forgotten in the eagerness of some to proceed with Japanese reconstruction at any price in order to stabilize the Japanese economy and institute a revitalized Japan as a counterbalance in the Far East to a Communist-dominated China.

General MacArthur also suffers the disadvantages of any man of his abilities and temperament; his immediate associates tend to become stuttering Charlie McCarthys, who are hardly even that. They only get things half right. A good example of that was the suppression by Major General Charles Willoughby, the Intelligence Officer of SCAP, of an editorial in the Nippon *Times* in October, 1946. The editorial was a sane warning to the Japanese not to supplant forbidden emperor worship by worship of some new god. The manner in which the Japanese, and especially the Japanese schools, were showing adulation for General MacArthur was not in the democratic tradition, it said. As an example of this attitude, the editorial cited the replacement in schoolrooms of Hirohito's picture with that of MacArthur. The children that had bowed reverently before the picture of the emperor now were doing the same thing before the glorified photograph of the Allied commander. The editorial writer didn't think this was a good idea.

An hour after the Nippon *Times* had started deliveries of its papers, General Willoughby and a group of MP's stormed into the newspaper's office, stopped the presses, confiscated what copies of the paper were still at the plant, and ordered the others picked up if possible. No explanation was given the Japanese, or even the American correspondents who learned of the suppression. Presumably, it was because Willoughby thought the editorial was disparaging of his chief and might lead to a lessening of respect and therefore of obedience to control. It could be that he thought it was perfectly all right for the Japanese to hold a reverential attitude toward General MacArthur. That would make him (Willoughby) one of the lesser gods to be worshiped.

The incident might never have become known—for the Japanese were afraid to talk about such things—had not Willoughby failed to have picked up the copies of the Nippon *Times*, containing the editorial, that had been delivered to the Foreign Correspondents' club; and had not Burt Crane of the New York *Times* staff been downtown late that evening and seen at the club a copy of the Nippon *Times* and the editorial. He made a mental note of it, intending to file a story the next morning with excerpts from the editorial to show that the Japanese did have an appreciation of democracy. He was surprised to see in the copy of the paper that was delivered to his home in the suburbs next morning that the editorial had been taken out. He made inquiries and learned what had happened.

The real stupidity of the whole business was that the Nippon *Times* had only reprinted the editorial from a Japanese-language newspaper. Several million Japanese already had read it when Willoughby mounted his white horse and dashed off to save his general from lese majesty. What his actions resulted in was the establishment of a well founded suspicion that American authorities did a lot of talking about democracy and about freedom of the press but that they didn't really believe in its practice. The incident also raised the suspicion in many correspondents' minds that similar stupidities may have been committed unknown to them.

It was a task for which there was no blueprint that the United States attempted when it sent its forces into Japan after the war: the peaceful redirection of the thinking of 80,000,000 people, the peaceful remaking of their character. All the disarming, all the changing of the economic structure of Japan will be of little use unless there is that far more fundamental change in the individual Japanese. There has been and there will continue to be disagreement as to just how this should be done, just how much of the old should be left and how fast the metamorphosis should be pushed. There should be no disagreement on some fundamentals, one of which would be the upholding of the right of the individual Japanese to express himself. No excuse that some of these expressions might tend to decrease respect for the occupying authority should be used to abridge that right.

This reeducation of the Japanese people is the most fascinating and the most difficult of the tasks undertaken by the occupation. For the very young the problem is fairly simple even if is immense. It is also the best hope for the future, as was pointed out by the Educational Mission, headed by Dr. George D. Stoddard, that went to Japan in the summer of 1946 to advise the Civil Information and Education Division of SCAP on its program.

"Sustaining as they [the Japanese children] do, the weight of the future, they must not be pressed down by the heritage of a heavy past," said their report to General MacArthur. "We would, therefore, stop wrong teaching but also, as far as possible, equalize their opportunities, providing teachers and schools to inform their minds without hardening their hearts."

Hitler and Mussolini proved that it was simple and that it was possible to mold the young mind. Neither embarked on his conquests until he had behind him a generation that had been educated in nazism and fascism, whose minds had been warped and whose hearts had been hardened while they were still malleable. The question whether the democratic way we are attempting to impose in Japan will be lasting depends on the 19,000,000 to 20,000,000 young Japanese in the schools. If they become convinced through their studies—by being taught not what to think but how to think—that our ways are best, then the future is secure.

The immediate program undertaken was to edit the textbooks, pending the introduction of new ones (the writing and the printing of which was an immense task for a school population of 20,000,000), and a screening of Japan's 450,000 teachers. It also included the placing in positions of responsibility of Japanese educators whose position had been proven in their opposition to the old methods of education by rote. How well the program has been put into effect is a matter of opinion. The answer lies somewhere in the future.

How to reeducate those beyond school age is a far more difficult job. Except for the favored few at the top, who were purged, the older people had learned from experience that aggression did not pay. "They were told when Manchuria was taken over that it would bring great prosperity to everyone," Premier Yoshida (then in his first government as premier) told me as we talked about Japan over the teacups in his office in the battered old Diet Building on a cold October day in 1946. "It brought most of the people only higher taxes. Manchuria led to China and finally to defeat."

Even if the older people of Japan, say those above forty-five or fifty, realize that, do they also realize what was lacking in their economic, political, and social structure that made it possible for a relatively small group of militarists and bankers and industrialists to lead Japan so docilely to disaster? It was Mr. Yoshida's belief that they do, that the great bulk of the people of Japan had been democratically inclined for a long time but that they had been misled. Granting the exactness of the premier's premise, there remains the large group of Japanese between fifteen and forty-five, on whom the immediate future must depend.

Under the prewar Japanese society it was very difficult for a young man to make himself heard. The Japanese social structure, built on the family, on the sanctity and the wisdom of age, was against the rise to prominence of a man ahead of his time, or on his merit alone. Age and conformity were worshiped. There was no place for youth and new ideas. This lower-age group, which includes the demobilized soldiers and the repatriated colonizers of Manchuria, China, and other conquered territories, is the group that must be sold the idea of democracy if the occupation-imposed reforms are to be more than transitory. The best, and about the only place, for them to gain quick prominence is in the labor movement. There the occupation record is both good and bad. The activity in the unions of Communists—who also saw the possibilities of the movement, as they do in all democratically ruled countries—gave antiunion forces in SCAP an excuse for interference.

In the early days of the occupation, labor organization was strenuously promoted by General MacArthur, who told prounion visitors from the United States that the democratic future of Japan was in labor organization. Unions that had been moribund for years under the emperor system burgeoned. When SCAP made its last detailed report on occupation in August, 1948, there were enrolled in 33,940 Japanese labor unions 5,129,693 men and 1,507,017 women.

The two types of labor organization familiar to Americans—craft and industrial, or horizontal and vertical as they sometimes are described—were explained to the Japanese and they were encouraged to form both, which they did. One is called the Japanese

Federation of Labor, which is an association of craft unions organized on the same pattern as the American Federation of Labor. The other is the Japanese Congress of Industrial Unions, which corresponds to the CIO in the United States. It has led in Japan to many of the intralabor conflicts that are prevalent in the United States and has mitigated against the influence of the labor unions in politics.

Because the Communists were a tight-knit group who knew exactly what they wanted and were ruthless in seeking it, they made great progress in the early days. It was they who led the newspaper strike of October, 1946, which failed when the workers at *Asahi*—Japan's largest newspaper from the standpoint of circulation—refused to join it. Communists also were in the forefront of the call for a general strike the second winter of the occupation for the avowed purpose of bringing about the fall of the first Yoshida cabinet. General MacArthur stepped in at the last minute to stop it under his broad directive to put down, by force if necessary, any movement that threatened peace and order or the successful carrying out of the occupation.

Three of the early Communist leaders were Kyaichi Tokuda and Yoshio Shiga, who had spent years in jail before and during the war and who were among the estimated 150 Communists released from prison along with other political prisoners when Allied occupation began, and Sanzo Nosaha, who had returned to Japan from China after sixteen years of exile. Nosaha is one of the few Japanese Communists who had been to Moscow. He was a member of the presidium of the Comintern.

The Communists were successful within the labor unions at first. But the SCAP crack-downs on strikes, or threatened strikes, that were openly Communist-led caused Communist leaders to lose face. They had concentrated on winning leadership of the key unions of transportation, communications, and information media. Passage of the National Public Service Law in 1948, which forbids strikes of government workers, struck at the very unions where they were strongest. The Public Service Law covers 1,700,000 workers in transport, communications, and public-utility fields. Organization in other unions of so-called "Democratization Leagues" clipped the wings of other Communist labor leaders.

Balked in union organization, the Communists apparently decided to concentrate on political organization, where they made substantial progress. They elected only five avowed Communists to the first postwar Diet, four to the second, but thirty-five to the third. From a membership of only a few thousand, their party rolls in early 1929 were believed to list a million or more. Over 3,500,000 Japanese voted on the Communist party line in the national elections of January, 1949.

The Japanese union member reacted erratically, if perhaps in a typically Japanese fashion, to his newly granted freedom. He was told by American instructors that the strike was labor's chief weapon; therefore he used it. He could be pardoned if he thought at first that SCAP was encouraging him to use it. He was not entirely happy with his new freedom, however. Under the old system he was treated virtually as a slave, working a twelve- to sixteen-hour day and with only two holidays a month (which was the system in the coal mines). But the employer at least had a paternal attitude toward him, keeping him on the payroll even if there was no work for him to do, and feeding him better under the old system than he was able to feed himself as a free man. He saw a questionable advantage in an eight-hour day and a five- or six-day week if he and his family went hungry, as many did when rice collections for the cities were below quotas.

One of the surprising needs that Premier Yoshida listed for his country, and which he said the United States could supply, was trained statisticians. Good statistics, he said, was one of the glaring lacks of prewar and wartime Japan. They had elaborate statistical services, I was told when I inquired, but they often concealed more than they revealed. Their crop estimates are a good example. Average fields in all areas actually were harvested to determine the exact yield. But then the local official would deduct a certain percentage because he feared Tokyo's demands would be too great. The next official up the line, knowing what had been done, would attempt to correct this deception which he was sure had taken place but at the extent of which he could only guess. When the reports finally reached Tokyo, no one could be sure just how close they had come to the mark. The Japanese thus never had the regard for figures that Americans have.

It will be a long time before Japan can be weaned away from her old ways. There is no doubt they are eager to change, for they can see in their ruined cities to what a state their old system led them. Even those who would like to return to power and to the old feudal system realize that the United States, using a different system, was able to defeat them decisively, so there must be some merit in political and economic democracy. Just how much they would like to imitate, however, remains a question in their minds.

There seems no question that Japan today is a more democratic country than it was before or during the war. Women do have the vote and they are exercising it. There are strong labor unions and many rising young labor leaders whose influence would have been small in the political parties but for their labor connections. So far, not so bad. If General MacArthur's health is sustained, if the United States does not attempt to move too fast in giving Japan back to the Japanese, if we do not begin to trust too much in the old political, military, and economic leaders in the belief we have a choice only between them and the Communists, then Japan may emerge some ten or twenty years from now as a democratic, peaceful nation. Or she might again become a predatory power, ready to make a deal with whomever would deal with her. If it were a deal to divide Asia, to whom would such men turn? To Washington or to Moscow? The answer is obvious. Only time holds the answer as to which it will be.

PART II. JAPAN AND KOREA

CHAPTER 3. *Land of the Morning Calm*

The old Korean phrase to describe their country translates freely as "Land of the Morning Calm." Today Korea is something considerably different. It is a land of disorder and indecision. The situation is one about which the Koreans can do little. Just as they were for forty years a chattel of Japan, so now they are a pawn in the game of power politics that the United States and the USSR have been playing since the victory was won.

Economically, Korea's problems are similar to those of Japan, with additional complications. The basic cause of these complications is the division of the country, which was begun when the United States and Russia divided Korea into zones of occupation with a closed border across which there was little intercourse. This division was perpetuated when rival governments were set up in South Korea and North Korea, each claiming jurisdiction over the whole land. The Republic of Korea was established in the South through free elections held under the supervision of the United Nations. It was quickly recognized by most of the non-Communist nations. The People's Democratic Government of the North was the outgrowth of the governing committee of Communists set up in the early days of occupation by the Red Army. It was recognized only by Russia, and the eastern European countries of the Communist bloc. Coincident with recognition, Russia announced withdrawal of her troops.

The only reason for division of the country was political. The South Korean area, which was the United States occupation zone and which became the Republic, is largely agricultural. North

Korea has 75 per cent of the industrial capacity, almost 100 per cent of the electric generating capacity, most of the anthracite coal deposits, and 95 per cent of fertilizer production. Under the Japanese, united Korea was an export nation, self-sufficient as to food. Divided, it is a deficit nation on both sides of the border. Lack of fertilizer has made it impossible for South Korea to raise enough food even for its own needs. North Korea has had to import most of its foodstuffs from Manchuria. When the Communist-created North Korean Government cut off in 1947 the electric power supply to South Korea in an argument with American Military Government, what industry there was in South Korea, which was largely textile mills, came almost to a halt until emergency generators could be sent in by the United States Army.

A further complication in the Korean situation was the decision to let the 600,000 Japanese who were repatriated from South Korea take home with them the fishing fleets which had furnished an important element in the Korean food economy. The Japanese also took home most of the technical knowledge that had operated so efficiently the Korean textile mills; and the Korean farm girls who had manned the mills, virtually as slave labor, scattered to the four corners of the land during the three weeks that elapsed between the surrender—when the Japanese opened the gates of the factory compounds and freed them—and the arrival of American troops. To get the mills back in operation, American occupation authorities had to start training operators, mechanics to keep the machines running, and even managers and bookkeepers.

Korea, even more than Germany, shows the difference between the United States and the Russian approach. When the Red Army moved into Korea from the Maritime Provinces and down to the 38th parallel—the dividing line between the two occupied zones—its commanders knew exactly what they wanted to accomplish, and they had a blueprint as to how to do it. Lieutenant General Hodge led the Twenty-Fourth United States Army Corps into South Korea with no specific orders except to maintain order. From that moment until Secretary of State Marshall dropped the

Korean problem into the lap of the unwilling General Assembly of the United Nations in the fall of 1947, the United States policy was one of improvise and compromise. Since there is no such word as "compromise" in the lexicon of the Kremlin, the Korean problem was doomed from the start to stalemate and to be a further irritant in United States and USSR relations.

The basic aim of both the United States and Russia undoubtedly was the same: to establish in Korea a government friendly to them. Guard Colonel General I. M. Chistiakov, the Red Army commander, had the formula worked out for him. He went in with enough troops—an estimated 300,000—to take control immediately of the whole of his area. He took in with him a cadre of Korean Communist leaders. All Japanese Army troops were disarmed and shipped off to Siberia as slave labor. Japanese civilians in North Korea were stripped of their possessions and chased across the border into the United States zone, where our Army had to feed them and see to their repatriation. Japanese civilian refugees from Manchuria were treated in a similar manner.

General Chistiakov and the Red Army then set about the organization of a Communist state in North Korea. From the very beginning they made it appear that the Koreans themselves were running their government—as undoubtedly they were. The Korean Communists who were placed at the head of the People's Democratic Committee—the ruling body—were well trained Marxists. All land, both that to which the Japanese held title and that held by wealthy Koreans—who by that very fact were damned without questions as collaborators—was confiscated and distributed among the landless sharecroppers. Foreign Minister Molotov told Secretary Marshall in the spring of 1947 that over 1,000,000 hectares of land (2,470,000 acres) had been seized thus and distributed without charge to 750,000 landless tillers. Because hunger for a bit of land to till is as old as Asia, that made heroes of the Communists to all but the landlords, of whom there were only a few anyway. The industries, which were almost all Japanese owned, were nationalized. The Russians, proving themselves wiser than the Americans, retained enough Japanese technicians to keep them operating in good order—that is, those which still could be operated after the Red Army had stripped them of what it was ordered to take home as "war booty." As in Manchuria, the equipment taken largely was electrical, of which there apparently is, or was, a great scarcity in Russia. Apparently enough was left, however, to insure a going industrial economy. Edwin F. Pauley, the United States Reparations Commissioner who made a Russian-escorted tour through North Korea and parts of Manchuria, estimated from what he saw that at least 90 per cent of North Korea's industry was left in working order, which was considerably more than the Russians left in Manchuria.

In contrast to the efficient, if brutal, manner in which the Red Army moved in to organize North Korea, the record of General Hodge and the United States in South Korea is a sorry one of muddling. Even the basic organization was wrong. General Hodge was both Supreme Commander in Korea and commander of the occupying troops. But an organization was set up to do the actual governing of the country—American Military Government—whose head was inferior in rank to General Hodge. (In Germany, the American Military Governor was the major authority.) To further complicate matters, the American arm of the Joint United States and USSR Commission that was authorized by the Moscow communiqué of December, 1945, to bring about union between the two occupied zones was headed by another United States Army officer, who also was inferior to Hodge. Theoretically, Hodge was head of the whole show. Actually, he was the least aggressive of the three high officers concerned, and the puzzled Koreans were presented with the confusing spectacle of three separate groups working often at cross-purposes. It was a situation of which some of the more adroit Korean politicians took full advantage, playing the three contending groups—they were even quartered in separate buildings—one against the other.

It was a terrific problem that faced both occupying powers. Korea is a nation of 30,000,000 people who were held virtually as slaves for forty years. Koreans had been given only minor places in government and industry during the forty years of Japanese overlordship. The Korean language had been forbidden; only Japanese was taught in the schools, and the young Koreans had to learn their own tongue secretly at home. There was only one opposition within the country, the Communists, who had been recognized by Moscow in 1923 and admitted to the Comintern three years later. The Koreans outside the country were thrice divided. In China was the Korean Provisional Government, which had been established in 1919 after the courageous Declaration of Independence by a small group of elders in Seoul in March of that year. In Washington was the Korean Commission headed by Dr. Syngman Rhee, who had fallen out with the group in China after having been its early leader. Dr. Rhee's main strength was his acquaintance with United States Government leaders. The third group was that of Korean Communists in China and in Manchuria.

With the Japanese surrender these three out-country groups began maneuvering for advantage. Inside the country the Japanese did as they had done elsewhere; they set up a provisional government which called itself the People's Republic. It was headed by a universally revered Korean named Woon Hyung Lyuh, who previously had worked with the Korean provisional government when it was in Shanghai. Although established by the Japanese and including some men who called themselves Communists, it was neither a Japanese puppet organization nor a Communist one in the sense that it had been directed from Moscow. Certainly it was as representative of Korea as any group that could have been quickly organized.

General Hodge, undoubtedly acting on general orders from Washington, declined at the outset to have anything to do with any of these groups, either inside Korea or outside. For over a month he declined even to see Mr. Lyuh. When he did, he was rudely insulting. As reported two years later by Mr. Lyuh, General Hodge's first question to him was, "What connections have you with the Jap?" His second was, "How much money did you receive from the Jap?" The answer to both was "None." Despite the denials, which apparently were sincere and honest, the general declined to have anything to do with Lyuh and his group. Instead, he started playing Korean politics, with disastrous results.

Even more disastrous than the general's political maneuvers, however, was his plan of operations "to maintain order." Even before he had landed at Inchon (the port for Seoul, the capital city), he had issued Communiqué No. 1, which was to the Japanese commanding general, ordering him and all Japanese "to hold their posts" and maintain order. The Japanese interpreted this so literally that when a group of joyful "liberated" Koreans went down to welcome General Hodge and the American troops, Japanese-led police fired on them, killing five and wounding many more.

The Koreans soon learned that General Hodge was out to maintain order at all costs, even if he had to use the Japanese to do it, that he was contemptuous of them and of their culture, that he had difficulty recognizing a barefoot democrat, and that because he did not speak their language, as did few of his staff, he was easily misled by the few Koreans who spoke English, most of whom knew that language only because they, or their families, had collaborated willingly with the Japanese during the forty years of Japanese occupation. Add to this the propensity of the general and his staff to see a Communist under every bed and it is little wonder that only a few months after the occupation many Koreans were muttering that it had been better "in the Japanese time."

After this initial stupid start, what was accurately called "government by interpreters" then set in. Directives began to issue in a stream from the various headquarters. Sometimes they were accurately translated. Sometimes they were not. One defining collaboration was so twisted in translation that only one or two persons in Korea would fall within its purview. Dr. Rhee finally was allowed back in Korea, as were the provisional government leaders in China, headed by the old revolutionary Kim Koo, whose chief claim to fame was that he had engineered the Shanghai bomb plot in 1932 which had resulted in the loss of a leg by the Japanese political leader Kijuro Shidehara. Shidehara was the one who, as foreign minister, stumped aboard the battleship *Missouri* in Tokyo Bay on his wooden leg to sign the articles of surrender.

With the return to Korea of the exiled political leaders began a wild scramble for power. It was both understandable and somewhat ridiculous. Anyone who could get the names of a few Koreans on his party rolls announced himself the head of a political party. For a country where political parties had been forbidden for forty years, this situation was not surprising. There were as many gradations from Right to Left in the hundreds of parties that materialized out of nothing as there were leaders. Gradually, however, the political alignments began to take shape. From Right to Left the Koreans coalesced around Kim Koo, Syngman Rhee, Kui Sic Kimm, Woon Hyung Lyuh, and Un Yung Pak, the Communist. There were many other lesser figures in between, but they proved relatively unimportant.

Instead of holding an election of some sort to let the various factions fight it out at the ballot box, General Hodge and his advisors finally decided to form a coalition government. Mr. Kimm and Mr. Lyuh agreed and became for a time the ruling favorites at headquarters. Mr. Koo and Dr. Rhee would have nothing to do with it. Mr. Pak eliminated himself, or rather was eliminated, by going into hiding to escape arrest. All Communist papers were suppressed. The Communist party disappeared as such, its members going into other parties or forming some new ones with the key words "Labor" or "Democratic" or "Patriotic."

Elections finally were ordered in late 1946, but for a legislative assembly only. It was a mockery of democracy. For one thing, only half the assembly was elected; the other half of it General Hodge appointed personally, with advice from his Korean advisors. This appointment business was undertaken, it was whispered, because otherwise Dr. Rhee's right-wing group—controlling the police and most of the provincial officials—would win overwhelmingly. The legislature proved as ineffectual as everyone thought it would. It was not even a good debating society. Mr. Lyuh was assassinated, presumably by Rightist bully boys, on July 19, 1947, and Mr. Kimm, who was legislative president, finally quit in disgust.

General Marshall's unhappy experiences in China attempting to bring irreconcilable forces together apparently had made him chary of success of any coalition movements in Korea. He made an effort in the spring of 1947, soon after he had become Secretary of State, to reach an agreement with Molotov on economic union of Korea. When that failed he laid the Korean case before the United Nations General Assembly. The U.N. appointed a Korean Commission to survey the scene and institute democratic government. The Russians walked out on the Assembly meeting and refused even to let the commission members enter North Korea. Elections were held in South Korea on May 10, 1948, however—and apparently honest elections—and the Rhee forces won. On August 15 the Republic of Korea was formally proclaimed, with Dr. Rhee as its first President. Transfer of authority to it from the Korean Interim Government—the euphemism describing the "government by interpreters" that had been the actual rulers of Korea for three years—went out of existence along with American Military Government. General Hodge returned home, a sadder if not a wiser man. He impressed me and other visitors to Korea who had some basis for judgment as an honest soldier who was completely out of his depth trying to run a country like Korea. He had, of course, few first-class aides, civilian or military. Korea was the Siberia of occupation.

Economically, General Hodge's reign was almost as inept as it was in the political field. All of the Japanese holdings were incorporated in a sprawling, inefficiency-ridden, graft-shot thing called the New Korea Company. It probably will take a full generation of Koreans to get its affairs straightened out. Instead of proceeding immediately to land reform, as the Russians had in the north, General Hodge waited until just before the elections sponsored by the U.N. in 1948 to announce a plan for distribution of land. As long as he had waited that long, he might as well have let it go a while longer and let the Rhee government take the credit for it. The plan, briefly, was to sell the seized land to tenants or landless peasants on easy terms to be paid out of the land. Whether it will work, only God knows. President Rhee publicly favored some such plan. What will happen when and if the new owners start to default on payments may be something else. Dr. Rhee is a strict businessman.

Despite all the blunders in Korea, despite the arrogance of some of the United States Army officials, the United States has come out of Korea with an over-all better reputation than have the Russians, although we left a weaker government in South Korea than the Russians left in the north. The North Korean land-redistribution program was a fraud. No firm title was given. The land remained the property of the state, subject to control by the local Communist committee, which could bounce the tiller any time it felt like it and for a variety of reasons. The brutality of the Red Army soldiers, who reportedly took what they wanted, whether it was women, rice, or factory equipment, alienated many who, like the Koreans in Seoul with the American Army, had first greeted them as liberators. In the first year of occupation alone more than 1,000,000 North Koreans streamed across the border to the United States zone, adding to the original disparity of populations—10,000,000 in the north and 20,000,000 in the south. Even with American bungling, the Koreans got the idea that our intentions were good. The big imports of American food were well publicized and there were just enough earnest, well meaning people among the liberators to show the Korean what could be done and to get at least a few of them started on the right road.

One of the departments which did much with little was that of Education, which was headed by my old University of Missouri classmate Lieuténant Colonel Aubrey O. Pittenger. By the end of the first year of occupation, there were 1,632,258 Koreans enrolled in school, with 31,342 teachers. The American plan of hot school lunches was instituted. There were no textbooks available in the Korean language. In the first year several basic textbooks were written in a simple twenty-four-letter alphabet, the type molded and set, and 4,800,000 of them printed on rough newsprint. It wasn't much, but it was a start. The Koreans were hungry to learn and the Education Department had the enthusiastic support of the educated Koreans and the Korean people generally. Education was something on which all factions agreed. It was something the Japanese had denied them for forty years, with the result that 75 per cent of the Koreans were illiterate. Another efficient group that worked unselfishly for the benefit of the Korean people were the Army doctors, who installed a laboratory to manufacture serum that stopped a bad cholera outbreak.

For the Koreans, liberation has been almost as great a tragedy as was Japanese seizure in 1905, a seizure, incidentally in which the United States Government, headed then by Theodore Roosevelt, connived at in the Treaty of Portsmouth. Imperial Russia escaped any great price for losing the war of 1904–1905 to Japan by giving Japan a free hand in Korea. President Roosevelt was supposed to have suggested that formula, being then a great admirer of the Japanese, an admiration that he later lost. The original mistake, of course, of the present impasse was made at Potsdam, in agreeing to a joint United States and Russian attack on Korea. It was the Soviet that blocked all efforts at unification of the country after the original division had been accomplished.

At the risk of being labeled a Communist, I might point out that there was some reason for Russian intransigence. They did not want an unfriendly government in Korea, as a future threat to their Manchurian holdings and their Maritime Provinces, with the vital port of Vladivostock. The men in United States Army uniforms with whom they had to deal on the Joint Commission, and the manner in which General Hodge ran South Korea, perpetuating the old Japanese police system and permitting Syngman Rhee's Youth Corps of young toughs to cooperate by beating up labor union members and leaders and terrorizing both city and countryside, gave the Russians no reassurance on the score of what kind of a government Korea would have if we had our way there. It would be a Rightist, anti-Communist government.

Whether it is ever possible to get along with the Russians or the

Communists, short of surrender, still is a moot point. Certainly, as the United States was represented in Korea, a compromise was impossible. South Korea does have now a democratically elected, if not a democratically inclined, government. The Koreans are proud, strong people. Students of their character do not believe they will submit readily to collectivization of farms or a police state generally. Predictions as to their future would be risky. One thing seems fairly certain: there is certain to be much trouble there between the two governments of North and South for a long time. Perhaps a form of government peculiarly Asiatic—neither completely communist on the Russian pattern nor completely democratic on the Western model—will evolve. If we support with our dollars and our technical knowledge whatever kind of government the Koreans themselves choose, they still may count the United States their truer friend. It should be possible to be pro-American without being anti-Russian.

PART III. CHINA

CHAPTER 1. *Sun, Chiang, and a Changing China*

When General George C. Marshall relinquished, in January, 1947, his effort to establish peace in China by bringing together the National Government and the Communists in a democratic coalition, he issued a statement as to why his mission had failed. "The greatest obstacle to peace," he said, "has been the complete, almost overwhelming suspicion with which the Chinese Communist party and the Kuomintang regard each other."

That went to the root of the matter, but it was like regretting an inability to mate a wildcat and a tiger. It was against nature for the two extremes to coalesce. The Kuomintang, as exemplified by Chiang Kai-shek, his family, and his family-in-law, and the C. C. Clique, led by the Chen brothers, had been since 1927 a ruthless dictatorship that had only occasionally established a façade of a people's government, and that largely for foreign consumption. Its policy was power, privilege, and profit. The Communist hierarchy was of just as tough fiber, just as ruthless as Chiang when the necessity was there. They too sought power. They were willing to see China prostrate to get it. One sought a dictatorship of the few. The announced ultimate goal of the Communists was a dictatorship of a few more. Added to this was a personal hatred that went far beyond the limits of political differences. Most of the top Communists escaped death only by chance in Chiang's purge of the Kuomintang in 1927. He always thought he was on their list of people who wouldn't be missed and had only struck first. To say that they were suspicious of each other was to understate the case. They hated each other like poison.

The reason the Communists finally won China was because they based their campaign on the people, the great, inert mass of 500,000,000 from whom Chiang and his inner circle had held themselves as remote since 1928 as does the Dai Lama from Western civilization. The Communists put their hopes in the political activation of the illiterate peasant and the underprivileged worker by promising him a change. Chiang put his hopes in a military campaign, financed by the United States, that would maintain the status quo. It was inevitable that in the long run the Communists would win. As any revolutionary movement will win that is led by resolute men who have faith in the people.

However the Communists may develop their government, they made their campaign for China's support against Chiang on a platform of free elections, freedom of speech, land reform, and reasonable working conditions for those in industry. Although Communist governments in other lands have adopted what might be described as permanent tutelage of the people, the Chinese Communists have abandoned that point of Dr. Sun Yat-sen's program and have promised the Chinese people an immediate voice in the selection of their officials. That is something they have never had in their three thousand years of written history. If the Communists let the principle become established, they may have difficulty progressing from that to the totalitarian rule that has followed successful Communist revolutions in Russia and in eastern Europe. There is at least a fighting chance that in China some form of democracy may emerge from the present travail to provide something better than she ever has had.

The civil war in China since the defeat of Japan has been depicted by many as a struggle primarily between the United States and Soviet Russia. That is nonsense. There is no question at all that United States support made it possible for Chiang Kai-shek to wage war on the Communists as long as he did. There is no creditable evidence I have seen, or heard of, that Soviet Russia has given any large-scale support to the Chinese Communists beyond abandoning to them the Japanese arms and ammunition that were taken from the 1,000,000 Japanese soldiers that were captured by the Russian Army and hustled off to forced labor in Siberia and elsewhere within the USSR. The Russian Army took out of Manchuria much war-potential equipment in the form of machinery and electrical equipment that would have made the Chinese Communist task much easier than it was had it been left there to produce for the Communist armies.

The USSR did not garrison any troops in Manchuria or North China to hold cities for the Chinese Communists; the United States did. The USSR did not fly any Chinese Communist armies to strategic cities; the United States Air Force did. The USSR, so far as it can be ascertained, did not send military missions to Chinese Communist territory to train their officers and men; the United States has had large military missions in China since the end of the war, advising Chiang and his military leaders. The United States turned over to the Chinese a sizable coastal navy, which the Nationalists used to good advantage in their campaigns against the Chinese Communists in Manchuria and North China, and it trained the men to handle them; the USSR did neither of those things. Some United States military men said the tactics used by the Communists when they began engaging in positional warfare with the Nationalists indicated they were receiving Russian military advice. The Communists received that long ago, under Chiang Kai-shek at the Whampoa Military Academy, which used Russian Army manuals as the training guides.

American apologists for the failure of Chiang Kai-shek and the Nationalist armies to crush the Communists in short order (which Chiang himself confidently told the inner circle of the Kuomintang in November, 1946, could be accomplished in six months) could see no other reason for the failure than that the Russians must be giving the Chinese Communists far more help than the United States was giving the Nationalists. They could not accept the other explanation, which was that Chiang himself was something less than the military genius he had been pictured, that his trusted generals were incompetent and corrupt, and that the morale of the Nationalist armies, and of the people behind them, was a minus and not a plus factor. Had conditions been what Chiang apparently hoped they were, his overwhelming superior military forces should have been able to break up the Communist forces within six months. When numerically superior and better armed armies with complete control of the air can be surrounded and "annihilated" as several of Chiang's armies were in the fighting of late 1948 and 1949, there is only one answer. Those armies are poorly led and the men do not want to fight.

The United States, from the end of the war with Japan in August, 1945, to late 1948, poured into Nationalist China more than $2,500,000 worth of military supplies, food, fuel, machinery, cotton, and technical advice. United States Marines garrisoned Peiping, Tingstao, and other smaller towns and guarded railway lines in North China for over a year. Through General Marshall Americans promoted a Political Consultative Conference that drew up a program of democratic reform and a plan for coalition government that could have brought peace, and perhaps even finally a real democracy to China. The PCC program was deliberately sabotaged by Chiang and his inner circle; no really democratic reforms were ever instituted in the Nationalist Government despite formation of a National Assembly and adoption of a constitution. At the end, Chiang was defeated. The description in some Government circles in Washington of our postwar China effort as "Operation Rathole" seems an apt one. What more could we have done, short of sending in an Army and taking over the civil war, to bolster a tottering regime?

The failure of the Nationalist Government to prevail over the Communists can be attributed only to one source, Chiang Kai-shek. During the twenty years that he ruled China as a dictator, he had many chances to lead China out of its hundreds of years of stagnation, to institute the reforms that would have robbed the Communists of all their propaganda points, to break the hold of foreign capital on many of her vital industries, to rally the Chinese people and world opinion behind him so that Japan would not have dared to attack in 1937. He was content instead to consolidate his own power and let his family and his wealthy backers enrich themselves at China's expense.

Chiang had this opportunity during the war with Japan when, during its early stages, the whole nation, even the Communists, rallied around him. During that period—until Soviet Russia itself was attacked by Germany and thus drawn into the "imperialist war"—Moscow was his chief source of supply and was not sending any supplies to the Communists at Yenan or elsewhere. He had the opportunity again during the period of Japan's war against the West, from December, 1941, to August, 1945; but the evidence is too overwhelming to be denied that during those years he was more intent on holding the Chinese Communists in check than he was either in fighting Japan or in instituting reforms within his own areas. He was able to defy all efforts at change by the threat to make a deal with the Japanese which would have freed at least 2,000,000 Japanese soldiers for use elsewhere against the Allies, perhaps even an attack on Siberia while the bulk of Russian armies still were engaged against Germany in the West.

It was not that Chiang did not know what should be done. Everyone else did. When William C. Bullitt, former ambassador to Moscow and Paris, went to China in the summer of 1947 for Henry Luce's *Life* magazine to promote the idea of sending General MacArthur to take charge of Nationalist forces and destroy the Communists, he came back with eighteen suggestions for Nationalist reform, none of which was adopted. Those eighteen suggestions were as serious an indictment of Chiang as could be drawn. They were:

1. Retire half the generals and a third of the other officers of the army—this being the number they consider incompetent or corrupt or both.
2. Cut the rolls of the army to one half; first, by removing all non-existent troops from the rolls; second, by disbanding units of the lowest quality.
3. Quadruple the pay of those officers and men who remain in the army and double their rations.

4. Punish severely all officers and men who, after having been given a living wage, graft.

5. Cut out all duplicate and useless government departments and agencies and dismiss all unnecessary government employees. It is estimated that this might reduce the government's civilian payroll by one-third.

6. Raise to a living wage the pay of those who remain, then punish severely all who graft.

7. Stop putting the government into industry and business, government ownership being followed inevitably by nepotism, inefficiency, and graft. Sell to the highest bidder those industries now under government ownership and genuinely encourage private enterprise.

8. Welcome foreign capital, in acts as well as words.

9. Decentralize the government, reducing military forces and military authority in the whole area south of the Yangtze to the absolute minimum consistent with national safety, returning authority to the civilian provincial governors and permitting the provincial governments to receive directly at least 25 per cent of the land tax and to make decisions with regard to provincial projects.

10. Reform the land tax and all other taxes and demand absolute honesty from tax collectors, under the severest penalties.

11. Hire foreign specialists to direct the reform of taxation, the collection of taxes, the revamping of financial policy, and the reconstruction of Chinese industry.

12. Compel all Chinese who have funds in foreign currencies or gold to deliver them to the government, and jail rich men who evade this measure or evade the full payment of their taxes.

13. Apply the draft law to the sons of the rich and the influential as rigorously as to the peasants.

14. Eliminate the draft exemption of students, and draft immediately all those students who are working on the side of the enemy in the present war—the Communists and fellow travelers who comprise about 5 per cent of the student body—and put them through a course of reeducation before sending them to the front. Permit patriotic students to make as many critical speeches and organize as many demonstrations as they wish.

15. Use Manchurians, as far as possible, in the administration of Manchuria.

16. Publish the exact facts about the Russian Red Army in Man-

churia, its rapings and pillagings, publication of which, in fear of Russia, has been forbidden. Also publish the abundant evidence of the subservience of the Chinese Communists to Moscow.

17. Publish facts on smuggling from Hong Kong into China, which is greatly reducing customs revenues.

18. Go through with the nationwide October and December elections, and, when the democratic constitution is in full force, end in reality as well as name the period of "tutelage" by the Kuomintang inaugurated by Dr. Sun Yat-sen in 1924.

"A program of this sort would unquestionably be popular throughout China, and with some American assistance it can be carried out," Mr. Bullitt added.

When a critic as friendly to Chiang as Mr. Bullitt considered necessary reforms as fundamental as most of those, it shows a bankruptcy of government almost beyond redemption. Especially, when to those defects are added an unsound currency and a dictatorial attitude which would neither listen to criticism from within or from without, nor accept it.

Mr. Bullitt's estimates of what help Chiang Kai-shek would need from the United States if the suggested internal reforms were adopted were: assignment of General Douglas MacArthur as military commander of all Chinese forces, training and reequipment of thirty Chinese divisions at a total cost of $600,000,000, spread over three years; the advance to China of $600,000,000 of credits for commodity purchases and of $150,000,000 for currency stabilization. Since, up to the time he made his assessment, in late 1947, the United States had poured more than $2,500,000,000 into the sievelike pockets of the Chinese Government, and had offered Chiang just as good military advice as MacArthur probably would have been able to give, Mr. Bullitt's estimates seem naïve, to say the least. What was needed to defeat the Communists was internal reform. And this was never carried out.

The only really hopeful period in China since the Japanese surrender was in early 1946 when, under Marshall's urging, a truce was agreed on between the Nationalist Government and the Communists, and the PCC, which included also the middle group in China represented by the Democratic League—a loose coalition of small parties and individual liberals—met and worked out its five-point program of reform and cooperation.

The five major decisions of the PCC were:

1. reorganization of the government along multiparty lines instead of the one-party (Kuomintang) government that it had been since 1928;
2. adoption of a common platform;
3. convocation of a National Assembly;
4. drafting and adoption of a constitution along Western lines;
5. reorganization of the army on a 5–1 basis (five National Army divisions to each Communist division).

What happened to that agreement was fairly described by General Marshall in the public report he made on January 7, 1947, of the failure of his efforts to implement the five decisions of the PCC. He said then:

I think the most important factors involved in the recent breakdown of negotiations are these: On the side of the National Government, which is in effect the Kuomintang Party, there is a dominant group of reactionaries who have been opposed, in my opinion, to almost every effort I have made to influence the formation of a genuine coalition government. This has usually been under the cover of political or party action, but since the party was the Government, this action, though subtle or indirect, has been devastating in its effect. They were quite frank in publicly stating their belief that co-operation by the Chinese Communist Party in the Government was inconceivable and that only a policy of force could definitely settle the issue. This group includes military as well as political leaders.

On the side of the Chinese Communist Party, there are, I believe, liberals as well as radicals, though this view is vigorously opposed by many who believe that the Chinese Communist Party discipline is too rigidly enforced to admit of such differences of viewpoint. Nevertheless, it has appeared to me that there is a definite liberal group among the Communists, especially of young men who have turned to the Communists in disgust at the corruption evident in the local governments—men who would put the interest of the Chinese people above ruthless measures to establish a Communist ideology in the immediate future. The dyed-in-the-wool Communists do not hesitate at the most drastic measures to gain their end as, for instance, the destruction of communications in order to wreck the economy of China and produce a situation that would facilitate the overthrow or collapse of the Government, without any regard to the immediate suffering of the people involved. They completely distrust the leaders of the Kuomintang Party and appear convinced that every Government proposal is designed to crush the Chinese Communist Party. I must say that the quite evidently inspired mob actions of last February and March, some within a few blocks of where I was then engaged in completing negotiations, gave the Communists good excuse for such suspicions.

However, a very harmful and immensely provocative phase of the Chinese Communist Party procedure has been in the character of its propaganda. I wish to state to the American people that, in the deliberate misrepresentation and abuse of the action, policies and purposes of our Government, this propaganda has been without regard for the truth, without any regard whatsoever for the facts, and has given plain evidence of a determined purpose to mislead the Chinese people and the world and to arouse a bitter hatred of Americans. It has been difficult to remain silent in the midst of such public abuse and wholesale disregard of facts, but a denial would merely lead to the necessity of daily denials; an intolerable course of action for an American official. In the interest of fairness, I must state that the Nationalist Government publicity agency has made numerous misrepresentations, though not of the vicious nature of the Communist propaganda. Incidentally, the Communist statements regarding the Anping incident which resulted in the death of three marines and the wounding of 12 others were almost pure fabrication, deliberately representing a carefully arranged ambuscade of a marine convoy with supplies for the maintenance of Executive Headquarters and some UNRRA supplies, as a defense against a marine assault. The investigation of this incident was a tortuous procedure of delays and maneuvers to disguise the true and privately admitted facts of the case.

Sincere efforts to achieve settlement have been frustrated time and again by extremist elements of both sides. The agreements reached by the Political Consultative Conference a year ago were a liberal and forward-looking charter which then offered China a basis for peace and reconstruction. However, irreconcilable groups within the Kuomintang Party, interested in the preservation of their own feudal control of China, evidently had no real intention of implementing them. Though I speak as a soldier, I must here also deplore the dominating influence of the military. Their dominance accentuates the weakness of civil government in China. At the same time, in pondering the situation in China, one must have clearly in mind not the workings of small Communist groups or committees to which we are accustomed in America, but rather millions of people and an army of more than 1,000,000 men.

I have never been in a position to be certain of the development of attitudes in the innermost Chinese Communist circles. Most certainly, the course which the Chinese Communist Party has pursued in recent months indicated an unwillingness to make a fair compromise. It has been impossible even to get them to sit down at a conference table with Government representatives to discuss given issues. Now the Communists have broken off negotiations by their last offer which demanded the dissolution of the National Assembly and a return to the military positions of January 13 which the Government could not be expected to accept.

Between this dominant reactionary group in the Government and the irreconcilable Communists, who, I must state, did not so appear last February, lies the problem of how peace and well-being are to be brought to the long-suffering and presently inarticulate mass of the people of China. The reactionaries in the Government have evidently counted on substantial American support regardless of their actions. The Communists by their unwillingness to compromise in the national interest are evidently counting on an economic collapse to bring about the fall of the Government, accelerated by extensive guerrilla action against the long lines of rail communications—regardless of the cost in suffering to the Chinese people.

The salvation of the situation, as I see it, would be the assumption of leadership by the liberals in the Government and in the minority parties, a splendid group of men, but who as yet lack the political power to exercise a controlling influence. Successful action on their part under the leadership of Generalissimo Chiang Kai-shek would, I believe, lead to unity through good government.

In fact, the National Assembly has adopted a democratic Constitution which in all major respects is in accordance with the principles laid down by the all-party Political Consultative Conference of last January. It is unfortunate that the Communists did not see fit to participate in the Assembly since the Constitution that has been adopted seems to include every major point that they wanted.

Soon the Government in China will undergo major reorganization pending the coming into force of the Constitution following elections to be completed before Christmas Day 1947. Now that the form for a democratic China has been laid down by the newly adopted Constitution, practical measures will be the test. It remains to be seen to what extent the Government will give substance to the form by a genuine welcome of all groups actively to share in the responsibility of Government.

The first step will be the reorganization of the State Council and the Executive Branch of Government to carry on administration pending the enforcement of the Constitution. The manner in which this is done and the amount of representation accorded to liberals and to non-Kuomintang members will be significant. It is also to be hoped that during this interim period the door will remain open for Communists or other groups to participate if they see fit to assume their share of responsibility for the future of China.

It has been stated officially and categorically that the period of political tutelage under the Kuomintang is at an end. If the termination of one-party rule is to be a reality, the Kuomintang should cease to receive financial support from the Government.

That was General Marshall's explanation. The Democratic League had another. In its report, also issued in January, 1947, it laid primary blame for failure on the noninclusion of Manchuria (which was still partially occupied by the Russian Army in January, 1946, when the truce was negotiated, since Moscow did not get all its troops out until March 10) in the truce agreement. This report said, in part:

We all remember that an hour before the opening of the Conference [PCC, January 10, 1946], the Kuomintang and the Communist Party, through the efforts of General Marshall, signed a truce agreement. This was welcomed at the time as great news for peace in China. Unfortunately, the underlying cause to the failure of the PCC Agreement was also to be found in this truce agreement. Namely, Manchuria was ruled out of the sphere in which the truce was to be carried out. In other words, the Government in its eventual armed "recovery of sovereignty" in Manchuria was not subjected to the restrictions of the truce agreement. Owing to this exceptional provision in the truce agreement, Manchuria became a suspended case in the two-party struggle, and a key factor in the continuation of internal strife. The Democratic League was the first to express its opposition to this provision in the truce agreement. For we consider that the peace of the nation, like the peace of the world, is indivisible. Nor can it be divided territorially. If the two-party conflict is to be solved at all, it must be solved once and for all and in its entirety. No loop hole should be permitted to exist in any area for party strife to rekindle. It is regrettable that this view of ours was not seriously considered or accepted by other participants in the Conference.

To be perfectly frank, both the Kuomintang and the United States Government had their own special reasons for leaving the Manchurian problem out of the cease-fire truce. In Manchuria, while the Kuomintang was planning an anti-Communist campaign, the United States Government was seeking to establish a *cordon sanitaire* against the Soviet Union. These two policies supplemented each other. There was a joint Kuomintang–United States policy. As a consequence, the already complex situation in Manchuria became even more of a tangle. It became not only a burning national issue but also an international one. After the Japanese surrender, the government continued to send to Manchuria large bodies of troops with the United States Government taking charge of their transportation. This was really uncalled for. Later on, the U. S. Government harbored the design of long-term garrisoning of North China by American troops. The Democratic League called for the withdrawal of American troops as early as 1945, for we knew then that the Northeastern problem would one day become insoluble. The truce terms were signed on January 10, 1946. In March and April, armed conflict broke out anew in Manchuria. It spread to China proper; local conflict soon turned into national war. The American mediator General Marshall became helpless in the face of this worsening situation. The root of all this could be traced to that single provision in the truce agreement with all its implications. The fight in Manchuria became the signal for the continuation and extension of the armed party struggle in China. In the view of the League, the sacrifices and devastation that the nation has sustained since are altogether meaningless and avoidable.

The hopes that General Marshall expressed, that the National Government would be reorganized in fact as well as in name, did not materialize. There was an outward show of reorganization, a few of the minor parties were given minor places in the government, the expanded Legislative Yuan became more outspoken at times in its criticism, but there was no fundamental change in the one-party and one-man rule of China. Emergency powers were granted to Chiang Kai-shek, and matters went on as they had until the bankruptcy of the Chiang Government was shown in the collapse of 1948–1949 and Chiang's retirement on January 21, 1949.

I was in Yenan in November, 1946, just at the time when negotiations in Nanking finally were breaking down. Fighter planes from Sian (American P-51's that had been turned over to Chiang) were making daily reconnaisance flights over the Communist areas. Nationalist ground armies were only fifty miles away. Heavy fighting was going on in Manchuria, north of Mukden, and extensive guerrilla activity was being carried out by the Communists elsewhere. On the flight from Peiping to Yenan our plane had passed over a village on the railway only some fifty miles south of Peiping which the Communists had raided and set afire the night before. It was still burning. Yenan itself was being evacuated of all equipment, government records and women and children.

It was in that atmosphere that I submitted eleven written questions to Chairman Mao. Two days after I had submitted them I was told that General Chu Teh would answer them, the chairman being too busy to see me at the time. With Lu Ting Yi, the Central Committee's Director of Information and Propaganda (a rather young-looking man who was dressed in Western clothes and spoke good English), acting as interpreter, General Chu Teh and I talked for an hour in the unheated meeting hall of party headquarters, on the back wall of which hung portraits of Stalin, Chiang Kai-shek, President Truman, and Prime Minister Attlee. (Elsewhere in Yenan the usual combination was Stalin, Roosevelt, and Churchill.) Following are my questions, and General Chu Teh's answers, as I noted them at the time:

Q. What effect will the convening of the National Assembly in Nanking have on further negotiations for peace? [The Communists had announced their intention not to participate.]

A. The determination of Chiang to hold a National Congress will mean a further disruption of national unity.

Q. Would the withholding of further military aid to Chiang Kai-shek by the United States bring a quick end to the civil war? Or has the aid already extended given the Nationalist armies a superiority of arms that the Red armies could not overcome?

A. The aid already given Chiang Kai-shek is sufficient for prosecution of a full-scale war for one or two years. Weapons, however, cannot decide all. During the last few months of fighting we have annihilated thirty-five Nationalist brigades. [He explained that the usual brigade was of about 5,000 men.] In these operations we have seized much United States equipment. It is very good. We hope to get more of it. [The last statement was followed by a broad grin.]

Q. It has been reported that Li Li San [the Communist exile who had returned to Manchuria with the Russian Army and was political commissar for Lin Paio's armies in Manchuria] may be following in Manchuria a different political line than that of Yenan, one closely tied to Soviet foreign policy. Do you know if that is so, or is he operating there under your direction?

A. It is not true that Li Li San is operating independently of Yenan. He is operating there under the direct control of the Central Committee here.

Q. Would a change now of United States policy in China be sufficient to remove the bitterness, expressed in Red China through the campaign now being conducted through the newspapers and by posters?

A. The people of all China are bitter at the United States reactionaries. There is no bitterness between our people. You have experienced none here, have you? [I told him I had been met only with smiles and at least outward good will.] Our Government makes it clear that our bitterness is toward your Government, not toward the American people. They understand the difference.

Q. If, by force of arms or by persuasion, a unified government was formed in China, what would be the attitude of the Communists in that government toward the United States? Would it be one of cooperation, or of distrust?

A. No unity can be established by force. That is a historical fact. The future attitude of the Communists depends on the attitude of the United States Government. The Hurley incident [Ambassador Hurley's recommendation against military aid to the Communists during the Japanese War and his lecturing of Mao and the other leaders during a flying visit to Yenan] and events of the last few months have not built up trust in the United States Government.

Q. Do you have any direct ties with Soviet Russia, as many people in the United States believe, or are you following in China an independent policy?

A. The Chinese Communist party always has pursued an independent policy.

Q. Have you [these questions were addressed to Mao] suggested recently to Chiang Kai-shek, or has he suggested to you, a personal meeting to discuss formation of a unified government in China? If such a meeting should be suggested from Nanking, would you accept such an invitation?

A. The chairman had a forty-day meeting with Chiang Kai-shek last year. We still have a delegation in Nanking.

Q. What basic differences still exist between the Communists and the National Government on formation of a coalition government?

A. We stand on the PCC decisions and the statements of the Moscow Conference [December, 1945]. They want to invite just a few Communists into the Government and the Kuomintang wants to use Communist troops only as garrison troops.

Q. Would the Communists accept a six-months truce now [previous truces had been limited only to a few days] and make a sincere effort during that period to decide differences on the political instead of the military level?

A. There is no reason for a war. There should be a permanent cease fire. The Communists have had bitter experience with previous truces. [He went on to explain how Chiang had used previous truces to redeploy troops.] We are willing to live up fully to the truce of January 10 [1946] if the Nationalists will restore the military position as of that date.

Q. Do you believe that General Marshall is sincerely striving for peace in China or that he is merely an instrument of an anti-Communist policy and of more aid to Chiang Kai-shek than to the cause of unity?

A. General Marshall must do what his Government tells him to do. He is restricted by his orders.

Q. Do you trust the motives of the Democratic League in its efforts to act as mediator between Nanking and Yenan? Has the League, in the last few days, offered any further concrete proposals for formation of a unified Government?

A. We do not distrust the League. There have been no new proposals.

Two days after that shivering talk with Chu Teh, Chairman Mao sent word that he would see me at tea time that afternoon. Accompanied by Bronson Clark, an American Field Service officer who was anxious to meet Mr. Mao, and Anna Louise Strong, the American woman writer (formerly married to a Russian Communist) who had arrived only two days before in Yenan and who invited herself along on the party, I forded the Yen River to Mr. Mao's cave apartment. After a cup of tea and some preliminary conversation, during which he said he had read my questions, and I asked him to speak generally and not restrict himself just to answering them, he talked, with few interruptions, for almost two hours.

Again Mr. Lu acted as interpreter, with Dr. George Hatem offering an occasional correction. I took no notes but Mr. Clark did. Following is my own elaborated version of the notes Mr. Clark took.

There is still hope [November 10, 1946] for peace in China. The solution lies in cooperation between the American people and the Chinese people. Not all Chinese and Americans realize this. Chiang uses some of them to fight a civil war. It will take time to awaken all the Chinese people to this truth. But it is certain to come. Only by a raising of the level of consciousness can a people understand the problem. The American people have given much aid to the Chinese people.

China has to perform many tasks that you have finished in the United States. [This was in response to a question about democratization of China.] Your problems are mostly because of your industry. Our problems stem from our backwardness.

There has been progress in understanding in the United States. More people now understand the situation here. The support given to Chiang is determined by your Government to the interests of the United States. It's not only a question of the USSR. In the latter part of the nineteenth century, before the USSR was formed, the Western powers supported undemocratic elements in China. Two instances of this were in 1850 and 1863. The Taiping Rebellion was ninety years ago. There was no USSR at that time. You also supported reaction from 1900 to 1917. All the Western powers were against Sun Yat-sen's democratic movement. It was not a question of the USSR then. The USSR now is only an excuse.

The character of the problem of Asia is always the same. The right wing of the capitalistic element wants to rule the world. United States monopoly capitalism wants to rule the world, including England. They have not yet got the USSR on the agenda. So some people want to find the USSR giving aid to Communist China. When they find no such aid, they are relieved. Then they see the truth and we make friends with them.

But not with the right wing of American capitalism. They know this is true [no aid from USSR], but they oppose us anyway. Regardless of the relations between the United States and the USSR, the right-wing capitalists oppose progress. Not only here, but all over the world.

Do Wallace [Henry Wallace] or other democratic forces in the United States receive USSR aid? Yet the right-wing capitalists oppose them. [He also mentioned Osmena and Roxas, the rival presidential candidates in the Philippines the previous year, but the connection was not clear.] There was no charge of USSR aid to the Communists when we were in the south. Now that we are in the north, they say we are getting aid.

We want to see the Roosevelt policy restored. In a few years this may be.

We don't want to lose Yenan, but if we have to we can carry on. The United States does not understand this method of recent fighting. Peasant reforms in our area lead the peasant to fight the National Government.

China's problem is not a local problem. It is a national problem. China cannot live on in the old way. United States policy now is against the interests and the will of the Chinese people. This policy will fail regardless of the Army, of the Air Force, or the loss of liberated areas, or the occupation of Yenan. We may have to suffer some losses but final victory does not belong to Chiang—it belongs to the Chinese people. The United States policy now is antagonizing the great majority of the Chinese people.

Whether Mao-Tse-tung was convinced of the exact truth of the charges he made against the United States capitalists and the United States Government, he made his charges with apparent conviction. It could be that he was quite sincerely convinced that there was a cabal in Washington that was intent on ruling the world. Neither he nor any other top Communist leader ever has visited the United States. We make it difficult for Chinese to come to our shores, except on brief visits. The immigration quota for 500,000,000 Chinese is one hundred a year.

It can be questioned whether Chairman Mao was completely honest in his belief that the Chinese would be able to make the distinction, when reading Communist propaganda against the Marines and other Americans in China, between the United States

Government and the American people. The woodcuts in the little Communist newspaper printed at Yenan, the *Liberation Daily*, depicted men in Marine Corps uniform running down peasants in jeeps, dragging Chinese girls around by the hair, and shooting Chinese workers. Posters on the public billboards that were at many crossroads repeated these lies about the Marines. Other Communists at Yenan, when challenged on the truth of this propaganda, admitted it might be overdone. Their answer always was, however, that there had been incidents such as were depicted and, besides, what were United States Marines doing in China helping to support the Chiang Kai-shek Government? How would we like to have foreign troops quartered in our country during times of peace? All the Japanese troops that had surrendered to us or to the Chinese had been repatriated by that time.

It was an illuminating experience to look at the United States, and at United States policy, through Chinese eyes. It was a picture considerably out of focus for an American, but apparently clear enough in its outlines to them. They cannot appreciate the interplay of political argument that is inherent in a democracy. They cannot appreciate the necessity of compromise that shapes so much policy, both foreign and domestic. Like us, too, they are inclined to believe what they want to believe. It apparently was widely believed at Yenan, for instance, that the Communist party in the United States was a strong political force, not the ragtag outfit that it is, a greater deterrent than a help to any reform that it joins in urging. They believed that it was Communist agitation that led to withdrawal of American forces from North China, not a sober realization on the part of the United States Government that our troops had no business there.

There seemed to have been in the United States an equally distorted view of the strength of the Chinese Communists. That is, there was until the Communists' dramatic military successes showed their strength and the weakness of the Chiang Government. The Chinese Communist party is not just a Moscow puppet. It is a revolutionary group that has placed itself at the head of a social revolution in China that has been going on for many years (as far back as 1850, as Mao pointed out). Dr. Sun Yat-sen is quoted more often than Marx in Communist China, the late President Roosevelt more often than Premier Stalin. Chiang Kai-shek was one of the leaders of this movement during the drive to the north out of Canton in the 1920's. But he turned his back on it when he broke with the Communists in 1927. When he attempted a grudging return to it in 1946 and 1947, it was too late. Some Americans in China believed he did not dare; that if he attempted any real reform he would be assassinated.

When Chiang Kai-shek climbed out of his bullet-proof limousine at the military airfield at Nanking on January 21, 1949, and walked without speaking past Vice President Li Tsung-jen, Premier Sun Fo, and other cabinet members and into his private plane to leave for exile, an era ended in China. It was a tragedy for China as well as for Chiang. A bold leader, a clever politician, a good administrator, he could have welded the great resources of his country into a great nation. But instead of making himself the servant of the Chinese people, he chose to make himself their master. They could have been led. They were too large a mass of humanity for one man to drive, no matter how ruthless that man.

It is this vastness of China and its problems that gives hope to many observers that a Communist dictatorship such as was established in Russia and, after World War II, in the countries of eastern Europe, is not feasible for China. The Chinese Communists do not have the trained political leadership, and particularly they do not have the technicians, either for government or for business and industry, that are so necessary in China. That means they will have to work for a long time with men who may not necessarily be opposed to them or to their program but who will be opposed to the reimposition of dictatorship—either of the Right or the Left—on China.

Soviet Russia does not have the things that China needs—machine tools, trained technicians, electrical equipment, even food. The United States does. The pressure will be for close economic relations with the United States and with Europe, particularly with the British. The Chinese must have in their government men who can deal with the West. They cannot eradicate all democratic leaders in China. The Chinese peasant himself, the world's greatest individualist, is not very fertile ground for regimentation—not when it is done without his consent. Whatever the Chinese Communist leaders themselves call their philosophy of government—the "New Democracy" or by some other term—it probably will be closer to our meaning of democracy than Russian communism. If we treat them fairly, there is no good reason why in ten years or so democracy may not be so firmly established that no small group of leaders can root it out. In the meantime it would be a very good idea for more Americans to know more about the Chinese Communist leaders and their program; not only what they say is their program but how it actually has operated in the areas they have controlled for years.

PART III. CHINA

CHAPTER 2. *Red China: the Men*

In December, 1927, when Mao Tse-tung, the chairman of the Chinese Communist party, and General Chu Teh, commander in chief of the Chinese Communist armies, joined forces at Chingkanshan, Kiangsi Province, in the south of China, they had with them only 1,000 men. Generalissimo Chiang Kai-shek's purge of the Communists from the National Revolutionary Government that had begun April 12, 1927, in Shanghai had reduced the Chinese Communist movement to isolated bands and single individuals in hiding. An estimated 140,000 of peasant and workers' leaders (not all of them Communists by any means in our understanding of the word) were killed in that blood bath and probably as many were jailed. Their blood fertilized the soil for a movement that now controls the world's largest country, a nation of 500,000,000.

Chiang's great mistake was that he did not kill Mao and Chu; Mao was captured and his wife was killed, but he escaped. It is possible, and even probable, that had those two been killed in 1927, the Chinese Communist movement still would have survived and flourished. It is an idea, as well as men. But it would hardly have survived in its present form. It is doubtful that it would, in twelve years, have become the ruling force in all China, as it has. For there is in Mao and Chu the qualities of leadership that have been able to carry it over obstacles that have effectively blocked other revolutionary movements.

Mao and Chu are totally unlike. Mao, the intellectual, is fine-boned, rather effeminate looking, quick of mind and action. He is affable. He laughs readily. Chu is like a block of granite. His light-blue eyes stare at you unblinkingly, as cold as those of a wild animal, belying the smile that occasionally breaks the weather-tanned brown mask of his face to show his strong white teeth. His walk is slow, deliberate, and ponderous. His progress through a group is like the movement of a flood crest in a river. Talking to him, that incredible long march of the Communists from south Kiangsi to northwest Shensi becomes credible, even inevitable. Here is a man, you feel, to whom no physical obstacle would seem unscalable.

With Chou En-lai (pronounced Joe En-lie), Liu Shao-chi, and Jen Pe-shih, Mao and Chu comprise the secretariat that has run the Chinese Communist party the last few years. Mao is, of course, chairman. Chu Teh is in charge of military affairs. Chou En-lai is in charge of foreign affairs, Jen Pe-shih of economic and financial matters, including taxes, and Liu Shao-chi of party affairs—the Jim Farley of China, to use a readily recognizable example. All were participants in the "Long March," a weighty distinction in Communist ranks. All, too, were early converts to communism and all held important posts in the Kuomintang before Chiang decided to exorcise his party of Communist influence. Their personal histories make up the history of the Chinese Communist party.

Mao, who usually is spoken of in Red China as "The Chairman" and not by name, was born in Hunan Province, in South China, in 1893. He was eighteen years old when Dr. Sun Yat-sen organized his revolt against the Manchus in 1911. Mao entered the Hunan Army as a private soldier. Army life was not for him, however, and he was in uniform only a few months.

During his army service Mao had decided to become a teacher. When he secured his discharge, he entered the First Provincial Middle School in Hunan and went on from there to the First Provincial Normal School, in Changsha, where he studied for six years. His political bent there began to show. In 1917 he helped organize the Hsin Min Hsueh Hui. Jen Pe-shih and Liu Shao-chi, his fellow members on the top secretariat, were fellow students.

After graduation from the Normal School, Mao went to Peiping (then called Peking) to continue his education at the National

University. It was there that he first came under the influence of Dr. Hu Shih, a former ambassador to the United States and one of China's fine liberals. It was there too that he met Yang Kai-hui, his first wife, who was killed by Chiang's men. They had a son, who is now a party functionary, educated in Moscow. Dr. Hu was so taken by the sincerity and the intellectual ability of the young Mao that he arranged for him to work in the university library to help pay his way through school.

The Bolshevik Revolution had swept Russia meanwhile and spread all through the world the seeds of worker and peasant revolution. Mao read everything he could find about that new (or old) venture in revolution and in government by the proletariat, and became a convert to communism. Leaving Peiping in 1919 he threw himself into the task of organizing China's students and indoctrinating them. A nucleus was his Normal School group, the Hsin Min Hsueh Hui. In 1921 he helped found, at Shanghai, the Chinese Communist party, which soon had flourishing Central Party Committees in five other cities. Branches later were formed in France, where many Chinese had been taken as laborers during and after the war, and in Germany and in Russia, in all of which there were large Chinese student groups.

Unlike some of the other Communist leaders, Mao entered the Sun Yat-sen revolution, and the Kuomintang, through the Communist door. All his work in the revolution, while the Communists were members in good standing of Dr. Sun's party of tutelage, was as a Communist. He was a Communist delegate to the first National Congress of the Kuomintang at Canton, in 1924. Those were the days when Chiang was a hero of the Red Revolution. Many newspapers in the United States which later praised him as the best bulwark against communism in Asia referred disparagingly to the generalissimo then as the "Red General."

While Chiang and many other early revolutionaries who later became the hard, corrupt core of the National Government in Chungking and Nanking were turning more and more to the bankers, industrialists, and landlords for advice, Mao and his fellow

Communists were at work among the peasants, the students, and the workers in the cities. Mao himself organized the peasant uprising in Hunan, in 1925, that failed and whose failure forced him to flee to Canton. There his talents were put to use by the Kuomintang, which made him Chief of Publicity and Propaganda. As such he was editor of the *Political Weekly*. During that time, too, he wrote many pamphlets. Even then, he was pointing out the differences there must be in Communist organization in China as distinct from Russia. It was the Chinese peasant, Mao saw, on whom the Chinese revolution must be based. Meanwhile, he was elected a member of the party's Political Bureau, the top Communist body in China as it is in Russia.

After a year in Canton, Mao returned to field organization for the Kuomintang-Communist alliance, first in Shanghai and then again back in Hunan among the peasants. In 1927 he organized in Hunan the Autumn Crop Uprising against the landlords and formed a Peasant-Workers' Army known as the "First Division, First Peasants' and Workers' Army." He was high on Chiang's purge list when the generalissimo decided to break with the Communists, and he was captured by Kuomintang agents. He bribed his way out of jail and fled to Chingkanshan, where Chu Teh joined him to form the "Mao-Chu" team that in their own lifetimes has become a legend among a quarter of the world's population.

Except for a brief period in that year (1927) when Mao disagreed so violently with party policy, which was being dictated by the Russian advisor Michael Borodin, that he was ousted from the Political Bureau and the party Front Committee, he has since been the head man of the Chinese Communist movement. After the uprisings counciled by Borodin had led to bloody defeat, culminating in the Canton Commune of December, 1927, what remained of the party rallied around Mao and Chu Teh.

In the cave city of Yenan and, after its fall to Chiang in early 1947, farther north in Shensi Province, Mao lived as the people with him lived, practicing what he preached. Everywhere in Red China, he had inscribed his personal slogan, "Serve the People."

And to serve them, he said, a government official must live as the people live, talk to them, study them so he may know what it is they want. Then when the government formulates a program, Mao says, it knows it will be accepted. What will happen, now that he is head man in China, only tomorrow's reporter can say. But as long as he is "The Chairman," it should be a good bet that the Chinese Communist leadership will not lose its contact with the people.

Grizzled General Chu Teh complements the intellectual Mao as a scabbard does its saber. Son of a wealthy family of South China, he always has been a professional soldier. He graduated from Yunan Military Academy in 1911 just as Dr. Sun's People's Revolt was beginning to gain ground in Canton. He commanded a company in the Yunan Provincial Army during the 1911 revolution; by 1916 he was a brigade commander. In that year he was named aide-de-camp to the governor of Yunan, which post he held until 1921 when, having become interested in the "New Movement" (communism), he decided to gamble his future with it.

In 1922 Chu Teh was sent to Germany by the Communist International to study the military strategy and tactics of the German General Staff in World War I and to help the growth there of communism. For his activities among the Chinese in Germany he was twice arrested by the Weimar Republic and finally was asked to leave Germany.

Returning to China in 1926 during the Kuomintang-Communist Entente, Chu Teh became first an army political commissar and then head of the Nanchang branch of the Whampoa Military Academy and chief of police of Nanchang.

When Chiang began his purge of the Communists, Chu Teh took over command of the Ninth Army at Nanchang and, with two other army leaders, led the Nanchang Uprising that was put down quickly by troops loyal to Chiang. With the thousand-man remnant of his forces, Chu Teh fled to Chingkanshan to join Mao.

Chu Teh is anything but the ignorant peasant leader that he has sometimes been pictured. He is a trained professional soldier and probably the world's finest tactician in guerrilla warfare. Since Nanchang he has never lost a battle with Chiang's men. The son of a wealthy family, he lived the life of a typical war lord for many years, with a fine home and many concubines. When he became fully converted to communism, he freed the latter and turned over his property to the party.

During his early military days Chu Teh became an opium addict. Instead of taking the "cure" under medical direction, Chu Teh cured himself by taking passage on a British boat, where the drug was not obtainable, and sweating out alone his desire for the pipe. There is nothing the elements, or man, can do to his body that he cannot take without a whimper.

Because of his age—Chu Teh was born in 1886—he has not been active in the field for many years, or even in active direction of the Communist armies. The little known Peng Yeng-huai, vice commander in chief, works out most of the plans. Chu is content to leave the military details to the younger men as he has turned more and more to political affairs. But Russian military textbooks that formed the basis for Communist Army doctrine have been so revised by Chu Teh and his staff through the years, from experience gained fighting the National Government armies and the Japanese, that they now could be said to be purely Chinese, which means largely Chu Teh.

Like Mao, Chu Teh lived simply at Yenan, sharing a small cave apartment with his wife of many years. He looked less like the commander in chief of armies totaling 1,500,000 men when I visited Yenan in November, 1946, than an aging coolie. He wore a faded, cotton-padded blue uniform without insignia, except for the Nationalist shield on his cap. (This was while the United Front that was formed with Chiang in 1937 to fight the Japanese was still ostensibly in effect and while the Communist armies in North China were still known as the Eighteenth Army Group, with Chu Teh as commanding officer.)

Unlike some of his younger colleagues, Chu Teh has no hobbies and few relaxations; but he was one of the few at Yenan who watched the American movies that were flown in from Peiping every week or ten days and shown nearly every night at the United States Army Truce Team headquarters, across North Valley, at Yenan, from Eighteenth Army Group and Communist party headquarters. Mao never attended the showings, but Chu Teh was a regular visitor, sitting impassively in the front row while Fred Astaire and Ginger Rogers danced and made love on an English sound track; while Fred MacMurray, Rita Hayworth, Barbara Stanwyck, and the other movie "glamour pusses" and "glamour boys" went through plots that must have seemed strange—to qualify for the understatement of the year—to this leather-faced old fighter who had lived with death and hardship as his constant companions for over twenty years.

Chou En-lai, the CCP's "foreign minister," and first Prime Minister of the Communist government at Peiping, is the most Western in dress, culture, and, probably, mode of thought of the top command. From 1938 to the final breakdown of negotiations in the winter of 1946, he was the Communist party's "ambassador" at Chiang's court. There he became acquainted with many Americans and Europeans, including ambassadors and newspapermen, and he took on a Western polish that was lacking among the men living in caves at Yenan. His intellectually and socially brilliant wife, Teng Ying-chao, rounded out a diplomatic team as suave as any in China's capital. Teng Ying-chao is an alternate member of the Communist Central Committee.

Chou, dark-haired, of medium height, quick in action, nervous, smiling, was born to be a scholar. That was 1898. He comes from an old and prosperous Mandarin family in Kiangsu Province. His father was an educator and his mother a student. The family moved to Manchuria in 1913, when Chou was fifteen, and his preparatory schooling was at Nankai Middle School, at Tientsin, from which he graduated at nineteen. He spent a year then at Waseda University, in Japan, but returned to Tientsin in 1919 to enter Nankai University. It was there that he became interested in revolutionary movements and began his study of Marx and Engel and Lenin.

Rich, handsome by either Chinese or Western standards, he soon became a student leader. His activities finally led, in 1919, to arrest and a year in jail. It was while serving his term that he met and fell in love with Teng Ying-chao.

Upon his release from jail in 1920, Chou went to France to continue his studies. He remained away from China for four years, studying in France, traveling in Germany and to England. All Europe was then in ferment, especially the student circles in which Chou moved, with the Communist idea that had achieved such startling success in Russia. Chou helped found the French branch of the Chinese Communist party in Paris in 1921. Its nucleus was the small group of Chinese students there and the coolies who had gone to France as laborers during the war.

Returning to China in 1924, Chou was made Secretary of the Provincial Committee of the National Government at Canton. A year later he became Chief of the Political Department of the Whampoa Military Academy, which Chiang Kai-shek had founded for Dr. Sun Yat-sen to train the military leaders of the revolutionary movement. When the Northern Punitive Expedition was organized to march on the Yangtze Valley and overthrow the rule of the Manchus, Chou was made political commissar of the First National Army commanded by Chiang Kai-shek.

As the revolution gained strength and spread northward, Chou was sent by Chiang to organize the Shanghai workers. This he did so successfully that by March, 1927, he was able to take over the city with his 600,000 organized men and turn it over to Chiang without a fight. This was the last cooperation among Chou, the Communists, and Chiang. A month after taking over Shanghai, Chiang began his purge of his Communist colleagues. Chou was arrested but, like Mao, contrived to escape. He fled to Hankow, where the Communists and the Kuomintang still were cooperating, and worked on the Military Committee of the National Government office there for a short time.

In August, 1927, Chou participated in the Nanchang Uprising that was led by Chu Teh and after the defeat fled to Canton, where he also took part in the Canton Commune, which also failed. Again he escaped death and for several months he went underground, working with Communist cells in Canton, Hong Kong, and Shanghai.

Chou went to Moscow in 1928 for the Sixth Congress of the Comintern, as representative of the Chinese Communist party, and was elected a member of the Communist International. In 1935, at the Seventh World Congress of the Communists, he was advanced to membership on the Executive Committee of the Communist International. He had returned, in 1931, through Chiang's blockade, to the Communist-held area of South China and he made the "Long March" to the northwest in 1934–1935. He was one of the Communist intercessionists in the "Sian Incident," when Chiang was kidnaped by the young Marshal Chang Hsueh-liang and, after much obscure negotiating, freed to return to Nanking. When the Japanese War began in 1937, Chou was sent to Chungking as Chinese Communist representative to the National Government, where he remained during the stages of that strange misalliance until November, 1946, when the negotiations, sponsored by the United States, for a coalition government finally broke down. Chou returned to Yenan then to join in the all-out fight that finally resulted in Communist victory.

The two other members of the Communist Secretariat—Jen Pe-shih and Liu Shao-chi—are less well known than Mao, Chu, and Chou. They were, like the other three, however, early converts to communism. Although several years younger than Mao—Jen was born in 1899 and Liu in 1898—they were schoolmates of his at Hunan First Normal School. Both were active in the revolutionary student movement there that was led by Mao, Liu being one of the staff of the little newspaper Mao edited there, the *Hsiang Chiang Comment*, the first Communist-slanted paper in China.

Jen spent most of his early years as an underground worker for the Communists. He organized in Shanghai, in 1921, the Communist Youth League, which he headed until 1927, when he became head of the Organizational Department of the Central Committee.

Jen went underground in Shanghai when Chiang conducted his purge and remained there for two years until ordered to Hankow to continue his organizational work there. He was arrested on suspicion by the Kuomintang secret police while enroute to his new assignment but was not recognized by them and after a month of imprisonment and examination was released.

An art student, and an artist of considerable ability, Jen opened a portrait-painting shop in Hankow as a cover for his real work. For over a year he operated from it an extensive Communist underground organization so skillfully that although the secret police knew he was in Hankow and carried on an unflagging search for him, they never linked the portrait painter with the Communist organizer, although many of his colleagues were caught and either jailed or killed. After a year, however, the trail leading toward Jen had become so warm that the Communist party leadership decided he had better change locations, so he closed his Hankow shop and returned to Shanghai.

Jen continued his organizational work until 1933, when he was sent to the western Hupeh-Hunan district to become political commissar of the Second Front Army led by Ho Hung. This army made up the rear guard of the "Long March," not starting for Yenan until almost a year after Mao and Chu had led the first contingent on the start of the long trek. When field headquarters finally were established in Shensi under Peng Teng-huai, Jen Peshih was made political commissar.

Jen did not become a member of the Central Committee until 1928 and was not elected to the Political Bureau until 1945, at which time he also became a member of the five-man secretariat in charge of economics and finance, which includes, of course, taxation policies.

Jen is one of the most approachable of the top Communist command. He gives the appearance of perennial good nature. Until a weak heart forced curtailment of his outside activities, he was an avid hunter, willing to walk for miles a day for one shot at the pheasants which are found in considerable numbers in the vicinity of Yenan. His main sedentary recreation is chess, which he plays well but does not take too seriously; he will argue loudly over disputed moves but finally gives in without rancor if he sees his opponent is adamant.

Liu Shao-chi, the party-affairs member of the secretariat, spent most of his early years as a Communist party functionary among the laborers, as distinguished from the peasants. With Li Li-san, who fell out with Mao Tse-tung in 1930 and spent the next fifteen years in Russia, Liu did the first Communist organization work among the railway workers, among the miners, and in the factories of the larger cities.

His first labor-organization task was in the coal mines of Honan and among the workers on the Peiping-Hankow railway. He and Li Li-san first organized the 10,000 workers of the An Yuan coal mines, with Li as secretary and Liu as one of his assistants. When the railway workers went on strike in February, 1920, as a protest against the Honan war lord Wu Pai-fu, the mineworkers, under Liu Shao-chi, left their diggings in a sympathy movement. Wu Pai-fu brutally suppressed the strike, killing many of the strikers.

When the Chinese Communist party was formally organized at Shanghai, in 1921, Liu was supposed to have attended as a representative from Honan, but he was so busy with his railway workers' union that he could not go and thus missed his chance to become one of the fathers of the party. His reputation was well known among the Communists, however, and when the China Labor Corporation was formed soon after the meeting of this first Chinese Communist Party Congress, Liu was named one of its top leaders. When, during the marriage of the Kuomintang and the Communist party, a General Labor Union for all of China was formed, Li Li-san was named its chairman and Liu its secretary.

As secretary of the General Labor Union, Liu continued his organization work. In 1924 he organized a strike against Japanese and British textile factories in Shanghai which eventually involved almost 300,000 workers. He was active, with Chou En-lai, in organizing Shanghai workers to seize the city and turn it over to Chiang in March, 1927. After the purge he moved the headquarters of the General Labor Union to Wu Han. It was at the Fifth Party Congress there the same year that he was elected to the Central Committee.

Liu spent most of 1928 and 1929 in Manchuria, with headquarters at Harbin, organizing the workers on the Manchurian railways, their paramount interest in which the Russians had formally abandoned in 1924 when they withdrew the Russian guards from the lines. That task done he moved south to Peiping to assume the leadership of the Hopeh Provincial Party Committee. Then back to Shanghai he went for two years in the underground Communist organization there and finally, in 1932, to Kiangsi, the "Long March," and his place as one of the Communist top command.

During the first period of the "Long March" he was party representative with the Fifth Red Army, then moved on to headquarters as department head of mass mobilization. After the Communists were well established at Yenan, Liu returned to Peiping as secretary of the North China Bureau of the Communist party. He remained even after the Japanese had taken charge in North China, in 1937, but finally left Peiping to join the New Fourth Army in the field as political commissar. He remained with it until 1943, when he returned to Yenan as secretary of party affairs.

Although there will always be a question as to who is the second man in a Communist organization—or any political organization, for that matter, where the top leader is as strong a character as is Mao Tse-tung or, to bring it closer home, as was Franklin D. Roosevelt—it is a fact that when Mao Tse-tung was in Chungking negotiating with Chiang Kai-shek in 1946, Liu was acting chairman in Yenan. Because of his close contact with party officials throughout China, Liu knows better than most what program will appeal to them and to the people; and his influence in shaping the party's program, and modifying it from time to time, has been great.

Like Mao, Liu has a personal enmity for Chiang Kai-shek that transcends the experience of most Western political leaders. His first wife, who was also a Communist, was liquidated by Chiang's men in 1934. Like Chu Teh, Liu came from a wealthy landholding family and became a Communist by intellectual decision, not because of inferior economic circumstances. His associates say he has no hobbies, that he is intense and logical in debate, and that he prefers to do his work at night, when the world is still and he can be alone with his thoughts. He lived at Yenan with his son by his first wife and with his second wife and their two children.

Li Li-san, who returned to China with the Russian Army in 1945 after fifteen years' exile in Moscow, is the son of a poor peasant family whose communism is glandular as well as intellectual. It was his rash program of continuous militant action against Chiang in 1929–1930, when the party was at its lowest ebb militarily, that led to his banishment from party councils. He had unseated Mao as leader in 1927 on such an issue, but his views did not prevail two years later. When the strikes he called among his personal followers in the cities resulted in disaster for party organization there, he was stripped of all titles and positions and went to Moscow. For many years in Communist circles any program that appeared too bold was generally referred to as the "Li Li-san line."

Li confessed his past errors in Moscow; and when he entered Manchuria with the Russian Army in August, 1945, he apparently was welcomed back with all sincerity and was appointed political commissar of the Democratic Unity Army in Manchuria led by Lin Piao, who is probably best known in the West of the Communist field generals.

Li is considered one of the best rabble rousers of the Communist leaders. He speaks Russian and French fluently (having gone to school for a time in France in the early twenties and having helped Chou En-lai organize the Chinese Communist party branch there) and can read English. His first two wives were killed by the secret police. While in Moscow he was married a third time, to a Russian woman.

Best known among the Communist leaders to Americans in China, aside from Chou En-lai, is Yeh Ch'ien-ying, who was Communist party representative at executive headquarters in Peiping during the futile effort of General Marshall to bring about a coalition in China. A professional soldier by vocation, he is a poet by avocation, writing in the Chinese classical tradition. He is sometimes referred to as the "scholarly general." Suave and polished in social contacts, as is Chou, he was a welcome guest with his daughter-hostess in American homes in Peiping during his stay there and inspired more trust among the top American command than any of his colleagues. "He is one Communist whose word you can depend on," said one top American general, who never hides his dislike for Chou En-lai for the very odd stated reason that he thought Chou had too great a fondness for the fleshpots of Nanking and Shanghai and was really a bourgeois at heart.

Yeh was born to a well-to-do family in Kwantung Province in 1897. Slated for training as a businessman, he was taken by an uncle to Malaya when about fifteen, but he did not like the tropics, nor business, and applied for admittance to the Yunan Military Academy. He passed the examination and went on to graduate from there with honors in 1920. He immediately joined the revolution under Dr. Sun Yat-sen, becoming a staff officer at military headquarters, where he so impressed on Dr. Sun his character and his ability that the Father of the Chinese Revolution made him his confidential secretary.

When Chiang Kai-shek began formation of the Whampoa Military Academy in 1924, Yeh participated in the planning and became Vice Chief of the Training Department when the academy was organized.

Yeh's first field command was as commander of a detachment of the Whampoa students who were sent out to subdue Chen Tsun-ming, war lord of Kwantung Province. His ability was highly regarded by Chiang Kai-shek, and Yeh quickly rose through several staff assignments to commanding general of a division during the Northern Expedition.

Whatever his thoughts and his inclinations may have been during this time, Yeh was not openly a Communist. But when Chiang began his purge of the Communists in 1927, Yeh refused to participate. Although now distrusted by Chiang, Yeh continued to hold commands under Chiang until December, 1927. Then, when ordered to liquidate the strikers in Canton, Yeh threw in with them instead and played a prominent part in the tragic Canton Commune. Now there was no turning back. Chiang ordered Yeh's arrest. Yeh escaped and went to Moscow, where he studied political and military science for three years in schools of the Communist International before returning to China in 1931.

During the "Long March," Yeh alternated with Liu Po-cheng as chief of staff to Chu Teh and as commander of the vanguard. When the Eighth Route Army and the New Fourth were organized in 1937 into the Eighteenth Army Group to war against the Japanese, with Chu Teh as commanding general, Yeh became chief of staff. He was elected a member of the Central Committee at the Seventh Congress in 1945.

Handsome, of medium height, Yeh is a charming guest, or host. In addition to his accomplishments as a classical poet, he also plays well the piano, the Chinese violin, and the flute. He reads both English and Russian, speaks the latter tongue fluently and English a little. He is married and has two sons and two daughters.

Except for Chu Teh, Tung Pi-wu, who was born in 1886, and Lin Po-chu, who was born in 1885, most of the members of the Central Committee of the Chinese Communist party are men in their forties, or early fifties. It is not illogical to assume that the rigors of life for a Communist in China since 1927 have contributed to this relatively young age level. The older men have long since gone to join their ancestors. The Communist top command are living examples of the operation of the law of survival of the fittest.

In addition to the Chinese, there was one strange man who walked for many years with the Communist high command, if he was not actually one of them, the Swiss-educated American doctor who, born in North Carolina, had been christened George Hatem but who had taken the Chinese name of Ma Hai-teh, and preferred that. He had abandoned a lucrative, if somewhat questionable, practice of medicine in Shanghai in 1936 to go into Yenan. He was, he said, only an unofficial medical advisor to the Communists and not even a member of the party.

A dark-complexioned, gray-haired man in his late forties, or early fifties, he was the unofficial greeter for all American visitors, an affable, apparently frank man, who lived at party headquarters exactly as the other top functionaries lived, dressed in Yenan-spun-and-made rough woolen clothes. He was treated with respect, and even deference, by the Communist leaders.

Many American visitors to Yenan during the truce days credited to Ma Hai-teh a much higher place in Chinese Communist councils than he would acknowledge. Although he said he did not read Chinese, he spoke it fluently and the English translations of many of Mao's writings were credited to him. He would have the Chinese read to him, it was explained, and then he would write down the English version.

He had married his former Shanghai nurse, a beautiful Chinese girl several years younger than himself; and when I was in Yenan, in November, 1946, they had one child, a handsome little boy of four years.

The Communists' long-time (1935–1947) capital city of Yenan, an incredible rabbit warren of caves dug out of the side of the loess hills 450 miles (as the plane flies) southwest of Peiping and some 3,500 feet above the level of the sea, is expressive of the hardihood of the Communist leaders and of the Chinese revolution they led. No government seat ever was closer to the soil than Yenan.

When the vanguard of the "Long March" arrived there in the fall of 1935 to set up shop, it was a small town of mud-brick houses within a great wall, forty feet high, some hundred feet thick at the base, and wide enough on top for a wagon road. It was known chiefly as a shrine city of the Buddhists, who had dug a temple out of the side of a hill and enshrined there some ten thousand images of Buddha, no two alike, or even of the same size. Pilgrims contributed the money for the statues on their visits. The names of the donors are carved below the Buddhas. The size of the statue is an index of the size of the gift. When the Japanese bombed the old town into rubble in 1938, the Communists took over the cave temple as a printing plant and for paper storage.

As more and more Communists converged on Yenan, until it became a city of some fifty thousand persons, the Communists spread out from the old city—which lies at the junction of three main valleys, through two of which flows the Yen River, from which the city took its name—into the adjacent valleys. Cave life was not new in North China, where the summers are hot and the winters cold, but nowhere else are they so extensive as at Yenan. They not only provide fairly comfortable living, they also are good bomb shelters. A man's home is his shelter at Yenan.

For obvious reasons the individual caves are small, about the size and shape of the interior of the Quonset huts made familiar to so many Americans during the war. Large caves would require roof supports, which are scarce. Connected by interior passageways, four make an apartment for top party leaders, twenty make a school or a nursery, and a hundred make a hospital. The front of each cave is covered by a latticework over which is stretched wax paper that keeps out some of the cold of the dry and windy winters. The flues from the cooking ovens that are built outside, under the overhang of the cave entrances, run under the floors or through the walls of most of the caves to an opening in the hillside. The warm air passing through these smoke ducts provides the radiant heating with which, in a somewhat different form, some modern homes now are being equipped in the United States.

This burrowing into the ground for shelter was not the only change the Communists made in the face of Yenan. Because the narrow valleys did not provide enough arable ground to provide the food for such a large concentration of people in that part of China, the Communists began cultivating the hilltops and planting winter wheat on slopes that a burrow could hardly climb. Flying into Yenan, the first visual evidence that the city is near is the contour-plowed hilltops with their fuzz of green. Despite the fact that the rainfall, of a yearly average of fourteen inches, is concentrated in the spring and early summer months, the method of plowing to follow the contour of the land, and the strips of grass that are left untouched, seem to have minimized the erosion one would expect from cultivation of such steep slopes.

This city of caves, which stretches for miles up the large valleys and into many of the smaller ones, is connected only by narrow, undrained dirt roads and horse and camel tracks. In the dry weather they are knee-deep in dust; when it rains they are knee-deep in mud. There is no need, however, for paved highways. The little Mongol ponies, who pull the big-wheeled carts or carry their masters aback in uncomfortable wooden saddles, seem to navigate the roads without difficulty. So do the big, splay-footed, long-haired camels, a caravan of which occasionally move slowly in from the north or northwest, as they have been doing for more centuries perhaps than our written history records.

The one thing Yenan does have, because of its altitude, is an invigorating climate. During the dry fall months, when the sun shines nearly all day, every day, Yenan has four seasons every twenty-four hours. It is wintry cold each night, coating the landscape with white frost and frozen puddles. Then the sun begins to get in its licks and by midday it is comfortable, in the sun, in shirt sleeves. When the western hills shut off the sun, the cold begins to come on again, and by ten o'clock skim ice is forming on the stagnant pools and backwaters of the Yen River.

It is an invigorating atmosphere, and place, in which to work. Although nearly all the normal appurtenances of government were lacking, with only radio and mule track as communication channels with the outside world, the Communists steadfastly clung to it as their headquarters. Perhaps the psychological advantage of such a capital outweighed its disadvantages.

The only Western note about Yenan was the forty-eight hundred foot-long air strip in East Valley that had been built by the Communists during the war as an emergency landing field for the China-based United States Army Air Force superbombers, the

B-29's. The Office of Strategic Services also established a modern weather station there, from which was sent out daily radio bulletins that helped the American bomber pilots on their flights to attack the factories in Manchuria. The airfield never was used during the war, but was used during the Marshall negotiations by the United States courier planes that flew the Communists back and forth from Yenan to Peiping, Shanghai, and Nanking, and kept supplied with gasoline, Diesel oil, chewing gum, and American movies the Army truce team that was stationed at Yenan to maintain liaison with the Communist leaders.

When Chiang's forces captured Yenan in the spring of 1947, in one of the Nationalists' last military successes against the Communists, the Kuomintang publicists in Nanking hailed its fall as a major defeat for the Communists. As a symbol, Yenan's loss was a blow to the Communists. Militarily, it was about as useless a victory as can be imagined. For one thing, it was hardly opposed. The previous November, both Mao and General Chu Teh told me they did not intend to make any large effort to hold the place. Before the Nationalist armies marched in, all Communist records had been removed, as had most other things of value, including the small rug factory and weaving mill that was there, the hospital equipment, and the families of all the Communist functionaries. It was a practically deserted city that Chiang's men found.

Yenan will never again, in all probability, be the Communist capital. It will always remain, however, as a symbol of the hard years of Chinese communism, and as the city where the Chinese Communist leaders lived for so long exactly as the people lived, where they erected with an idea and their bare hands an organization that finally came to rule the most populous country of our world.

PART III. CHINA

CHAPTER 3. *Red China: the Program*

When Mao Tse-tung addressed the Seventh Congress of the Chinese Communist party in the spring of 1945, he laid down a ten-point program that was adopted by the Congress as the official party line. Except for Point One, which called for the total defeat of Japan and was accomplished within a few months of the meeting of the Congress, it is believed to be the program the Chinese Communists have followed since and will pursue, at least externally, as the rulers of China.

The nine points remaining after fulfillment of the first were:

abolition of Kuomintang one-party rule and establishment of a coalition government;

establishment and guarantee of freedom of speech, assembly, association, thought, belief and of habeas corpus;

unification of the people (for peace as well as for war);

establishment of a true national army, not party armies;

reformation of land tenancy and ownership and division of all Japanese and traitor-held land among landless peasants;

encouragement of Chinese investment in industry with only such foreign-capital help as is necessary;

adoption of a program of adult education to wipe out illiteracy (estimated at 80 per cent in China) and encouragement of all forms of intellectual and cultural advancement;

guarantees of rights of racial and religious minorities such as Mongols, Mohammedans, Tibetans, and so forth;

establishment of cordial relations with all foreign countries, freedom for all colonial peoples, and support of all efforts to form and maintain an international organization to keep the peace.

This is a program with which most good lower-case democrats can agree, except perhaps with the proposed forcible division of the land. It is not state socialism. Especially is it not socialistic on the point regarding establishment of industry in China—which is its most radical departure from Marxism or Russian communism.

On that seventh of the ten points, here is the pertinent part of what Mao Tse-tung said:

> Under the new democratic state system, the policy of readjusting the relations and interests between capital and labor will be adopted. On the one hand, the interests of labor will be protected, and an eight- to ten-hour day will be adopted, according to different conditions, as well as appropriate unemployment relief, social insurance, and the rights of trade unions, and so forth. On the other hand, reasonable profit will be guaranteed for state enterprises, private enterprises, and cooperative enterprises under rational management. In short, both labor and capital will strive jointly for the development of industrial production.
>
> To develop industry, enormous capital is needed. Where will it come from? It can only come from two sources, mainly depending on the capital accumulated by the Chinese people themselves and at the same time borrowing through foreign aid. Under the condition of abiding by the laws of China and of being advantageous to the economy of China, foreign investments are welcomed. What is beneficial to both Chinese and peoples abroad are large-scale light and heavy industries and modernized agriculture in China which will vigorously develop after China achieves a solid internal and international peace, and a thorough political and agrarian reform. On this basis the field for foreign investments in China will be extraordinarily large. A China which is politically retrogressive and economically poor will be greatly disadvantageous not only to the Chinese people but also to peoples abroad.

Whether Western capital (which means probably only American capital today) will be attracted by a mere promise remains problematical, and will so remain for some time. It will largely depend on how the Communist-dominated Government of China conducts its affairs once it has consolidated its hold on the cities.

From 1927 until the military drive south and the overthrow of the Nanking Government, the Communists had confined their major activities to the countryside. Even in the preliminary stages of their final and successful effort to eliminate Chiang they by-passed the cities. They had no foreign trade, so they did not have to worry about foreign exchange or economic and diplomatic relations with the capitalistic countries. By cutting transportation lines and isolating the Nationalist-held cities of Manchuria and North China, they increased the problems of the Nationalist Government, which had the responsibility of providing food and fuel for them and, at the same time, decreased their own problem in the countryside. There was more than sufficient food there to feed the peasants if large portions of it did not have to be taken to the cities, so there was no hunger, at least, in Communist-held areas even if there was lacking many other things, including clothing.

This great problem of the governance of urban China as well as rural China, which the Communists acquired with their victory, gives hope that there may be mutations of communism there that will make it easier to deal with China on the Western pattern than many businessmen now think.

The major work of industrialization will undoubtedly, however, need to be done through government. The first great problem would seem to be the provision of power. That must precede the development of any wide-spread industrial plant, in either small or large units. With China's coal and oil resources limited or, at least, thought to be limited—scientific exploration of some of the more remote areas may reveal mineral resources not now even guessed at—development of hydroelectric projects is the obvious answer.

China has four major rivers, and many smaller ones, that could, if properly harnessed, provide the electric power for all the industrialization that China needs. Development of India's rivers was the first major project undertaken by the Indian Union after independence was won. A similar course undoubtedly will be followed in China. Since China herself has neither the trained technicians nor the electric equipment to carry through even a small-scale Tennessee Valley development, she must look outside her borders for both. The United States is the logical country. Soviet Russia has more projects of her own than she can handle for the next twenty years. The Russian Army's stripping of Manchuria of much electrical equipment shows what is Russia's great economic hunger.

Since as much as 60 per cent of dam building is manual labor, the problem is not as great in a country ruled by the Communists as it would be in a democracy. The Communists have no compunction about requisitioning human assets any more than they do about requisitioning land and capital. Manual labor, too, is never a problem in the East, where there are always more hands than there is work for them to do. The individual Chinese is capable of prodigious work on a diet on which a white man would starve. Hydroelectric development in China, therefore, would require only trained direction and certain specialized equipment from outside. It is not inconceivable that both would be available from the United States at a price China would be able and willing to pay.

How ready Western industrialists and businessmen will be to deal with a Communist-dominated China depends on what attitude the West will take toward the fact of a Red China which they cannot escape. There had been considerable evidence since the war that the British, who have much larger investments in China than have Americans or any other Westerners, had long since reconciled themselves to such an eventuality as a Communist victory in China and were preparing to meet it. They recognized the Communists as the legal government of China the first week of 1950. While Americans have been largely traders with China, without large capital investments (estimated at only $200,000,000 in 1940), the British own or have interests in railways, power plants, and many industrial establishments. Complete abandonment of China by United States businessmen would not entail the losses that the British would incur. When negotiations between the Communists and Chiang broke down in 1946 and early 1947, the British placed no barrier to the transfer of many Communist activities to the British city of Hong Kong.

The British have not had to take the onus of support of Chiang and are not as cordially hated by the Chinese as are the Americans. It was difficult to tell in 1946 and 1947 whether the Communists or the Nationalists hated Americans the more. Only the Communists openly carried on an anti-American campaign, but Chiang's government did little to halt anti-American demonstrations and many Chinese papers that were loyal to Chiang were bitterly anti-American.

There is the same question of implementation of the rest of the Communists' program, as laid down by Chairman Mao, as there is about that on industry and business. On Point Three—the democratic freedoms—he spoke only in generalities. He charged that all the democratic freedoms had been suppressed in Nationalist areas (which was only partly true) and that they were all protected in Communist areas (which was open to doubt). At Yenan there was a large Catholic church, which was the most imposing building in the whole area. To it, so the Communists said, came a priest once a month to hear confessions and give communion to the fifty or so Chinese Catholics in the area. From other Communist-held areas immediately after the end of the Japanese War came reports of deliberate persecution of all Christian sects, of the murder of missionaries, and the burning of churches. Other missionaries reported that they were not interfered with, although little was done to help them continue their work.

Despite over a hundred years of missionary work in China, the Christian religion has never been a very important factor there. The *World Almanac* credits only 3,260,766 professing Christians among China's 500,000,000. Of these, 618,600 belong to Protestant sects and 2,642,166 are Catholics. Mere membership of Christian churches is not a complete index to Christian influence in China, however. Through the Christian colleges and the Christian orphanages many more millions of Chinese people have been affected, both directly and indirectly.

Freedom of religion, if observed, could have a powerful effect on world opinion. Of this, it is believed, the Chinese Communist leaders are aware. They know that one of Chiang Kai-shek's strong political attributes for Americans was his confession of the Christian faith and membership in the Methodist Church, the largest Protestant group in the United States. Since so few Chinese actually would be directly affected, it seems reasonable to assume that the Communists, whatever they might think about Christianity, could afford to be tolerant of it.

The Foreign Missions Conference of North America, which includes sixty-one Protestant denominations, decided at its Buck Hill Falls, Pennsylvania, meeting in January, 1949, that it would take a pro-Christian and not an anti-Communist attitude toward events in China and would not withdraw its missionaries. As one of the conference leaders expressed it, he had "more hope than faith" in Communist promises to observe full freedom for all religions but that it was worth the effort to try and get along with them.

There always will be a place in any land for missionaries who can teach the people how to live as well as how to pray. Medical missionaries are welcome in all lands. That should be true especially in China, which never has had enough doctors or enough hospitals. This was recognized by the Buck Hill Falls Conference, which discussed the necessity of specialization for its missionaries in the China field. "Those [missionaries] who know a trade will be at a great advantage," said the Reverend Rowland M. Cross, secretary of the China Committee of the conference. "The boards are even considering the desirability of using celibate missionaries."

Dr. Frank T. Cartwright, China secretary of the Division of Foreign Missions of the Methodist Church, expressed what was the consensus of Protestant missionary leaders when he said that although there was some feeling that trying to work in a Communist country was "compromising with the Devil," that "most of us feel that if we are allowed to teach Christianity, or even live a life of Christian witness alongside communism, then we should do it." No missionary will be asked to stay in China, it was agreed, but those that do stay will be supported as long as they are there and as long as it is possible.

The Chinese Communist program that the Seventh Congress approved has been, so far as can be learned, followed through in Communist-held areas, or "liberated areas" as they called them. And even more than this formalized program, the various activities the Communists stimulated among the people—labor cooperatives, kindergartens, hospitals, orphanages, basic sanitation programs, discussion groups—must have given the people of the Communist areas more of a sense of belonging, of having a part in government, than they ever had under emperors, war lords, or the Kuomintang in its later phases. The Communist leaders were quite visibly of the people, living and working as they did. The peasants must have recognized that the Communist program was for their betterment. In their village, county, and provincial party meetings and discussion groups, they may even have acquired the feeling that government was by them as well as of and for them.

Yenan may have been just a showcase, and not representative of the rest of the Communist areas. If it was a showcase only, it nevertheless was a good one. In its kindergartens, primary schools, hospitals, its medical school, its university, on its agricultural experimental farm, in the near-by villages where sanitation programs were installed, the people seemed happier, more industrious, more enthusiastic than anywhere else in China. And the techniques used were certainly different.

None of the top Communist functionaries received any payment in cash for their services. Their needs were taken care of. The students in the schools paid no tuition but they did raise all their own vegetables and grains in fields set aside for them. The salaries of the teachers were figured on a commodity basis, so that fluctuations of the currency did not affect them. The higher ranking teachers at Yenan University, for instance, were paid 1 do and 8 ksings of millet per month. The instructors got half that. This was in addition to clothing, lodging, and food. The chancellor was Li Fu-jen, a former editor and educator of Sian who had been arrested, tortured, and left for dead by the secret police during the Chiang-ordered purge of Democratic League leaders in the spring of 1946. When I met Chancellor Li he still found it necessary to walk with a cane because of the bullet in his back that was lodged too close to the spine to be removed with safety. He was not a member of the Communist party.

The sanitation program that had been formulated by Dr. Hatem and that was practiced in Yenan and, supposedly, elsewhere in Communist China, was so elementary that it might appear foolish to an American living in a steam-heated house with indoor plumbing. It was a program of ten simple rules: drink only boiled water, separate the privy from the house, have at least one window in each room, bathe at least twice a week and change to clean clothing, do not sleep at night in the same clothing worn during the day, and so forth. While the people were becoming accustomed to this regime, Dr. Hatem said, he encouraged them to post a list of the rules on the wall of their houses and check off each item as it was fulfilled.

The International Peace Hospital at Yenan, which was one of seven in Communist areas that had been partially furnished by money provided by Mme. Sun Yat-sen's China Relief organization, had to be, by necessity, almost as elemental in its approach as was Dr. Hatem's sanitary code. It was largely set up in caves, at different levels on a steep hillside. Patients brought their own bedding. The beds themselves were just wooden planks. The operating theater was one of the few buildings. It was octagonal in shape, with six outside fireplaces to provide the high temperatures necessary inside. On the operating days—which were Tuesdays and Thursdays—the fires were started early in the morning. "It works very well," Dr. Hatem said.

They had few drugs from outside and used many ancient Chinese herb medicines, which they prepared themselves at the hospital. Even many of the instruments were homemade, although two Russian doctors, who had been in the Red Army in Manchuria, recently had come in with their army operating kits. "These were a godsend," said Dr. Hatem, fondling the shining instruments. Later General Gillem, the United States Army officer in charge of Executive Headquarters at Peiping, made two planes available to the American Friends Service Committee; and Bronson Clark, of Philadelphia, took in a field unit and several tons of supplies. There were no military patients in the peace hospitals. Despite the crude instruments and crude drugs, the lack of screens or X-ray machines or any of the other appurtenances of a modern hospital, Dr. Hatem said they had few infections. When I was there they had ninety patients—which was only half capacity, as Yenan then was being evacuated because the Nationalist Army was only fifty miles away—for whose care there were four doctors, twenty-six internes, seventy-one nurses, and forty trainees. Dr. Wei I. Chia, a graduate of Cheloo Medical College, Shantung Provnice, was the directing head of the hospital and the chief surgeon. Dr. Wei said that typhoid, typhus, and a relapsing fever called Kalaazar brought in the bulk of the cases. The hospital charges no fees, although the families of patients contribute food.

The hospital was administered in connection with the medical school, the curriculum of which was one and one-half years of continuous study. Trained doctors, by the standards of the West, hardly can be turned out in that time; but Dr. Hatem said the need for physicians of any sort was so great that they could not take longer. In their course of study they do learn considerable preventive medicine, some rudimentary surgery, and how to prevent infection in childbirth. The death rate in the Yenan area, in 1937, had been 64 per 1,000 adults, Dr. Hatem said, 500 per 1,000 infants and 25 per 1,000 maternity cases. In 1946 it was 37 per 1,000 for adults, 218 per 1,000 infants, and no maternity deaths. Rapid extension of these rural hospitals and of these elementary medical schools is high on the list of the Communist program for all China.

Probably the most valuable, and most difficult, of the tasks of reeducation of the Chinese people that the Communists had undertaken, and which they can be expected to continue, was that of cooperatives. These were not just the consumer cooperatives that are familiar to Europeans and Americans but labor cooperatives as well. In even the smaller villages the menfolk were organized to work together. If one needed a house, all would set to work to build it. During the slack agricultural season they would hire out as a labor gang for work on the roads or on some project in the nearest town or city.

One of the complaints of most Americans who have had long contact with the Chinese is that they do not know how to work together. One Chinese will strain to place on a cart a load too heavy for him. Another alongside him will be straining at a similar task. They found it difficult to accept the idea that two lifting together could place the two burdens much more easily. To the Westerner accustomed to the "team" idea from school days all this seems stupid, and it is. But it is a custom hard to break. A little incident that occurred one day on a road east of Yenan shows that even in Communist China the idea has not yet been completely sold. A pack train of horses and burros was bringing coal into Yenan from a mine. One of the train was a small burro attended by a boy who appeared to be no older than ten or twelve years. When the train was stopped for a minute to let a United States Army truck pass, the small burro slipped in the mud and fell. His load of two large baskets of coal was too great for him to lift and to regain his feet. His young driver appealed vainly to the others to stop and help him. They passed unheeding. When two of us who were in the truck helped the little burro to his feet, there came a roar of laughter from the other drivers and an incredulous babble of thanks from the small boy.

The administration of justice in Communist areas was almost as elementary as the cave housing. Its organization in the liberated area of Shensi-Kansu-Ningshia (which was one of eight into which Communist China was divided at that time and which was ruled from Yenan) was similar to the Western pattern. In the three provinces there were 30 local courts, 3 district courts, 4 subsupreme courts, and the supreme court at Yenan, which heard only appeal cases. The Chief Justice was Ma Su-woo, who had come up through the judicial system from a district court. He was not a lawyer by profession. He had provided the Communists with one of their newer folk songs in his ruling that a daughter did not have to accept her father's choice of a husband, a revolutionary doctrine in China. Chief Justice Ma had done this by voiding a marriage contract entered into by a girl's father with an elderly suitor and legalizing instead her runaway marriage to a younger man of her own choice. The Communist Propaganda Bureau wrote a song about the ruling.

All judicial posts, including that of the Chief Justice, are filled by election every three years. Chief Justice Ma was serving only his first term. The Associate Chief Justice, also in his first term, was Chon Soong-sang. He was a former lawyer in Peiping. The legal code of Communist China provided for no sentence longer than ten years and that all death verdicts must be by unanimous vote of the Supreme Court. Death sentences are carried out in the village or town where the crime was committed. All executions are public. Chief Justice Ma said death sentences usually were declared only in cases of proven, premeditated murder. The perpetrator of an unpremeditated murder may be sentenced to no more than one year's imprisonment. The relatively light sentences in most cases, Chief Justice Ma said, was because it was the Communist belief that imprisonment should be corrective and not punishment alone. They believe they can reform a man in a year or two. Ten-year sentences are unusual.

The prisons, unlike those in the Western world, are under the control of the Supreme Court. At Yenan the prison was only down the hill a short way from the series of caves that provided both the judicial chambers and living quarters for the court. The justices saw in prison, on their periodic visits, the men they had sentenced. Because of its isolation, there was little need for guards at the Yenan prison because few tried to escape; they could be too easily trailed and recaptured. The only bars were on the doors of the sleeping caves, which were as good as those anyone else had. The prisoners, like other residents of Yenan, raised most of the food they consumed. They also operated a cloth-weaving mill, making uniforms for the Communist armies.

The simplicity of life at Yenan hardly will be duplicated in an urban government seat. Governance of 500,000,000 people cannot be done from a cave or a cabbage patch. But these twelve years in the bare loess hills of Shensi Province must have had some effect on the character of the men who shared the hardships. Certainly it should have a large effect on public opinion over the rest of China when life in Yenan is well publicized, as it will be by the Communists. No government ever lived more simply. There has been no government in modern times that lived closer to the people than that of Mao Tse-tung and his fellow Communists of Yenan.

PART IV. FRANCE IN THE PACIFIC

CHAPTER I. *Indo-China, 1940 to 1945*

A few days before he assumed the premiership of France in December, 1946, Leon Blum wrote in *L'Populaire* that the problem of French Indo-China, where a strong nationalist movement had flowered since the Japanese surrender, was not one susceptible to solution by force. Among several members of the insurgent Viet Nam Government at Hanoi, Tonkin—the center of the freedom movement in Indo-China called Viet Minh—hopes were strong that M. Blum's ascension to power in Paris meant a peaceful resolution of their struggle with the colonial government at Saigon. Ho Chi Minh, the wispy little Annamite who was the head of Viet Nam and the leader of Viet Minh, was skeptical. He was talking to two traveling American press correspondents in the bedroom of his suite in the former French governor general's palace. They asked him if he did not believe that M. Blum's statement and now his position in the French Government was not encouraging for peace.

"A man will often say as a private citizen what he would not do as Premier of France," said President Ho prophetically.

A week later the uneasy truce that had prevailed since the previous spring when the Viet Nam leaders and Jean Sainteny, Republic Commissioner for Tonkin and North Annam, had signed at Hanoi the March 6 accord that would have made Indo-China a free country in a French Union, erupted into open, bloody war. The fighting began when French soldiers were ordered to remove the barricades the Viet Namese had erected around their part of the city. The Blum government was contradicting his own prediction. The French were temporarily successful. Ho Chi Minh and the

Viet Nam Government were driven out of Hanoi and their followers from most of the other cities of Tonkin and North Annam. But from the countryside they harried every French line of communication, infiltrated the cities in civilian clothes to toss grenades in open windows, ambushed any French force that dared to venture far out of the cities. In two and one-half years the French lost ten thousand dead, twice as many wounded. Hundreds of their impressed Foreign Legionnaires—largely former German soldiers recruited from prison camps—deserted to the Viet Namese or escaped across the Siamese or Chinese borders to lose themselves in Bangkok, Canton, Hong Kong, and Singapore.

What practically every informed neutral observer had predicted would happen had happened. The French troops and colonial administrators were pinned in a few cities; the economy of the country was prostrate. Since the end of the war France has poured hundreds of millions of dollars into an attempt to reimpose colonialism in Indo-China and has failed. It was not until the French set up in 1949 a nationalist Indo-China Government under Bao Dai, the former Emperor of Annam, to which they gave greater autonomy than Ho Chi Minh had been promised in the 1946 Accord that there was any weakening of support for Ho.

France's handling of Indo-China through the years, and especially since the war, is so excellent an example of colonialism at its worst, of the exploitation of an Asiatic country by a European power, that it deserves a telling in some detail. The action of the white colonial there is one of the principal reasons why communism has made such important gains in Asia since the war. A prolongation of such policies which depend, in the final analysis, on United States support is a sure way to guarantee that all Asia some day will be Communist and the "yellow peril," which the jingoist Hearst press screamed about for years, will be a reality.

Indo-China is a relatively young colonial area. Although French explorers were early in the Pacific, along with the Spanish, Portuguese, British, and Dutch, it was not until 1862 when the King of Annam ceded Cochin China to France that the French began to take active control of the country. A protectorate was declared over Cambodia in 1862, over Annam and Tonkin in 1884, and over the sparsely settled western Kingdom of Laos in 1893. Those five areas—Cambodia and Laos, inland, and Annam, Cochin China and Tonkin, abutting on the South China Sea—comprise French Indo-China. Cambodia today has a population of about 3,000,000 and is a constitutional monarchy under French protection. Laos also is a monarchy under French protection. Its population is estimated at 1,000,000. There are freedom movements in both states but there has been little real trouble in either. The other 26,000,000 of Indo-China's population live in Cochin China, Annam, and Tonkin—which all originally were under one king—and it is these three over which the Republic of Viet Nam claims authority and where the war has been waged since August, 1945.

From the earliest days of conquest the French made little pretense of ruling Indo-China for other than the purpose of enriching their own pockets. The latter, however, they did right well. The southern part of Indo-China is one of Asia's rice bowls. Before the war exports from there averaged better than 1,500,000 tons a year. From the northern regions were exported coal, cement, and other minerals. Except for a few British and American oil companies, practically all business in Indo-China was a French monopoly. This included the highly profitable opium trade, which is going full blast again throughout Southeast Asia today. Before the war, Indo-China is estimated to have yielded annual net profits to the French Government and to French interests of as much as $300,000,000. It required only a few Frenchmen to mine this rich lode; the *Statesman's Year-Book* for 1937 gives the French civilian population of Indo-China as 30,711 and French troop strength there as 31,000. More troops were not needed, for the people of Indo-China are, or were, as nonbelligerent as the Indonesians under 350 years of Dutch rule. They had been exploited too long and too harshly by their own leaders to feel any great hostility to French methods.

In eighty years of colonial administration the French built two beautiful European-style cities—Hanoi and Saigon—constructed some 2,000 miles of railroad, made Saigon and Haiphong modern ports, and established schools in which the 7,000 children among the 30,000 French could secure an education, from kindergarten to the *lycée* level. For the Indo-Chinese it was something else. There were over 6,000 schools and 400,000 pupils, but most of these were only primary schools teaching the three R's. After eighty years the literacy level was only about 10 per cent.

Supreme economic authority of Indo-China was the Bank of Indo-China, a French institution whose marble headquarters in Saigon is as fine and ornate a building as any banking structure in Europe or in the United States. Its upper windows look down on a river as crowded with sampans and misery as in Soochow Creek in Shanghai. The palace of the governor general was cool and spacious, set in a great park surrounded by a high iron fence. There were lovely modern homes and apartment houses in the French section, kept immaculate by Annamite servants. In a square near the center of tree-shaded Saigon is a beautiful playground for small children. There every day patient little Annamite nursemaids took care of the white children who frolicked in dresses imported from Paris. French colonials in white shirts and shorts and sun helmets sipped hot coffee and cool drinks and bought peanuts from ragged little vendors outside the open-air café of the Hotel Palace-Continental. The hotel has modern bathrooms and great canopied beds that make it believable that perhaps Marie Antoinette may have slept there.

French Indo-China was the first stopping place for the Japanese when they began moving south in 1940, preparing for the attack on the Philippines, Malaya, and the Netherlands Indies. The men of Vichy were in command in metropolitan France and they had their counterparts in Indo-China. The French garrison at Langson offered token resistance when the Japanese landed at Haiphong and moved up the River Rouge in the fall of 1940, but that was all. Saigon became Southeast Asia headquarters for Count Terauchi, commander in chief of all imperial Japanese forces in that area, and remained so until the surrender of August 15, 1945.

During all the years when the American, British, and token Dutch forces were fighting the desperate battles of Corregidor, Bataan, the Java Sea, Guadalcanal, Iwo Jima, Leyte, and the rest, French colonial administrators and French soldiers were collaborating with the Japanese to squeeze from Indo-China the last possible pound of rice, ton of coal, sack of cement to help Japan try to win the war. It was not until March, 1945, that the French began to get restive under the impact of the news, brought them surreptitiously, of American victories and of the bombs that began to fall on Saigon from the B-17's and the dive bombers of Admiral Halsey's Third Fleet fliers. Then they were interned by the Japanese along with other former Axis nationals. Freed by the Japanese surrender, they calmly began setting up again the old colonial system.

Because of their inferior numbers, the French in Indo-China had the excuse that opposition to Japan would have been futile. But according to the Annamites the collaboration was more than perfunctory. It seemed to them to be wholehearted. Like Laval and others in metropolitan France, many of the French in Indo-China apparently thought they were lining up with the winning side.

During these war years the only underground in Indo-China was that maintained in the northern state of Tonkin by Annamites led by Ho Chi Minh. These cooperated with agents of the American OSS led by Major General Bill Donovan, and with Army and Navy sea-air rescue teams who penetrated much of Southeast Asia and South and East China to pick up and return to American lines fliers parachuting from damaged planes. Japanese forces were spread so thinly through most of the areas that these underground movements operated in the countryside with little interference.

In the other countries of Southeast Asia, nationalist leaders were used by the Japanese to provide a façade of independence and local sovereignty. This was true in the Philippines, where a Republic was proclaimed, in Indonesia, in Siam (where the Pibul Songram Government was left in power), and even in China, where a puppet government was set up under Wang. In Indo-China—until March, 1945—the Japanese had the French Colonial Government as their puppet administrator. The only native collaborators were those who had worked with the French before the war, principally those attached to the various captive thrones.

Although the French first raised the cry of collaboration against Ho Chi Minh, as the Dutch did against the Republicans in Indonesia, it quite obviously was a charge that had no substance. Ho Chi Minh had been a revolutionary since he was a boy—his parents, allegedly, both had been executed by the French in 1910—and he never treated either with the French or with the Japanese. It was not under Japanese orders, nor even under their benevolence, that he and his followers declared the Republic. They already held de facto control over several of Tonkin's provinces before the Japanese surrender and had been so active there for years that it required a full Japanese division to keep open supply lines and repair the railroads and the bridges that the guerrillas led by Ho Chi Minh constantly harassed and cut.

On August 19, 1945, four days after the surrender, Ho Chi Minh declared at Hanoi the establishment of the Republic of Viet Nam, with himself as President. People's Committees were set up in other cities. Emperor Bao Dai abdicated his throne on August 30 at his capital city of Hué, in North Annam, and was taken into the Republican Government as a principal adviser to Ho Chi Minh under his more common name of Citizen Vinh Thuy.

How sincere was this act of abdication, when Bao Dai handed over to Tran huy Lieu, as representative of the Republic, his golden seal and his ruby-incrusted golden sword, remains to be seen. In accepting at Paris in March, 1949, the offer of the French to back him in an attempt to set up in Indo-China a national government in opposition to that of Ho Chi Minh, he did not demand back his throne. He was quoted at the time of his abdication as saying, "As long as I remain on my golden throne, I am a mere pawn in the hands of the French." Bao Dai never was very active in the Republican Government after his abdication despite his title of Adviser to the President, and soon left the austerity of North Annam for the more pleasant life of Hong Kong, where the French first opened negotiations with him in 1947 on a promise of restoring to him his ancient kingdom.

Meanwhile, at Potsdam, Premier Stalin, President Truman, and Prime Minister Attlee had decided that British and Chinese troops would be sent in to accept the surrender of the Japanese in Indo-China and to restore order there. (There were no French forces available in the Pacific to do the job.) The Chinese were to occupy the northern part of the country, from the Chinese border down to the 16th meridian; the British were to take over the task south of the 16th parallel. The Chinese sent in one division, the Ninety-third, from Kunming (whose absence permitted Chiang Kai-shek to take over rich Yunnan Province, which he had long coveted). The British also sent in one division, under Major General Douglas Gracey, made up largely of Indian troops.

The British and Chinese troops, taking up their duties—defined as repatriation of Japanese and maintenance of order—late in August, found the whole country in the firm control of the Viet Minh leaders and everything in order. There had been no mistreatment of the interned French soldiers or civilians, the latter being allowed back to their homes. The Republic had established itself at Hanoi and elsewhere; People's Committees were functioning under recognized leaders. If these men were either Japanese puppets, as the French first charged, or Communist stooges, the first American, British, and French correspondents into the country could not detect it. They appealed to them as Indo-Chinese nationalists, whom their French masters had not attempted to defend against Japanese aggression and who believed now that they were going to be allowed to run their own country. They were soon disillusioned.

The Chinese in the north gave de facto recognition to the Republic, quickly disarmed and repatriated the Japanese soldiers and kept the French in the internment where they had been placed the previous spring by the Japanese. They plucked the banks, the people, and the land like locusts, contributing to the famine that had begun a year before when the Japanese converted many rice fields to castor-bean culture because they needed the oil more than the rice and were unconcerned as to how many Indo-Chinese might die. (The Republic says 2,000,000 died in one year; others say that total was twice the actual number. Even 1,000,000 would be staggering—one in twelve of Tonkin's population.) They completed their mission and departed in four months, leaving Ho Chi Minh and Viet Nam in complete control.

General Gracey, in the south with headquarters at Saigon, acted much as did his counterpart in Indonesia. He did not immediately molest the People's Committee which had taken charge of the city and was running its affairs smoothly, but he declined to have formal dealings with them. He made no immediate attempt to disarm or intern the Japanese, merely kept them in their camps, but fully armed. When French Colonel Cedile arrived with 150 commandos, he permitted him to reform and gradually rearm the 5,000 French soldiers whom the Viet Minh leaders already had released from internment. When Colonel Cedile, on the morning of September 23, moved to oust the People's Committee and take back control of the city, the British made no effort to stop him, and British and Japanese troops soon joined in the effort.

The Viet Minh leaders and forces, taken by surprise, were driven from Saigon, but they continued their resistance in the countryside. A general strike was called in Saigon and most of the Indo-Chinese left the city. The French in Paris, meanwhile, were clamoring for transportation to take their troops back to Indo-China; it was a rich prize they had no intention of losing. Looking around at their own devastated country, they longed for the rich profits which had flowed from the French colonies in Asia for so many years. Soon British and American ships were unloading shiploads of French soldiers, many of them in American uniforms they had worn in France, at Indo-Chinese ports. By the turn of the year there were an estimated 50,000 of them in Indo-China, and the British withdrew. The long colonial war to restore the former French monopolies was in full swing.

PART IV. FRANCE IN THE PACIFIC

CHAPTER 2. *Uncle Ho and the Viet Minh*

The French Sûreté has a heavy dossier on a little Annamite revolutionary dating back to the early 1900's. Until the war the dossier bore the name "Nguyen Ai-Quoc." In Annamese that means "Nguyen the Patriot." Since 1945 it has borne the additional notation "Alias, Ho Chi Minh." The little Viet Nam leader neither confirms nor denies that the two are the same. There is little doubt of it, however. The Sûreté's files carry pictures of Nguyen Ai-Quoc. For my eye the pictures of Nguyen Ai-Quoc and the mental picture I carry of Ho Chi Minh, propped up in bed in Republican headquarters in Hanoi on a chilly afternoon in December, 1946, are of the same man. Whatever the name, the President of the Republic of Viet Nam is the leader, the brains, the conscience of the nationalist movement in French Indo-China.

Much has been made of the fact in the United States and in Europe that Ho Chi Minh is an assumed name. It is recited as though it were an unusual circumstance in Asia for a man to change his name, which it is not, and as though it had been done in his case for a criminal purpose. Much more has been made of the charge that Ho Chi Minh is a Communist and that the Viet Minh is Communist-dominated.

To the question as to whether he is, or was, a Communist, Ho Chi Minh's answer is a qualified affirmative. "Yes, I was a Communist," he once told a questioner. "But I am no longer one. I am nothing but a member of the Viet Nam family." Other members of the Viet Nam Government who worked with Ho Chi Minh both before and during the war probably would make the same answer. Among the Executive Committee of Viet Minh in Cochin China there was only one avowed Communist, its followers told me. On the committee also was a native Catholic priest. The Communist party, as such, was dissolved in early 1946, when Ho Chi Minh decided that there should be no political division within the Viet Minh, at least until independence had been won.

In the United States (or in any established democracy) whether a man is a Communist, or whether he was one and has publicly recanted, is an important guide to his character. That man once made a choice between democracy and communism. It was one he was free to make. In Asia, and especially in colonial Asia, adherence to communism has a considerably different connotation. For the revolutionary in the 1920's—when Ho Chi Minh allegedly was Comintern agent for all Southeast Asia—the choice was subservience to colonialism or adherence to communism. Moscow was the world's only revolutionary capital, the only place to which the revolutionary could look for any practical help—or even ideological help. His pleas were neither heard nor answered in a Conservative-led England (itself a large colonial power), and certainly they were not heard nor heeded in the United States of Harding, Coolidge, and Hoover.

Whether Ho Chi Minh was a Communist, or still is one, is not greatly material to the situation in Indo-China. It could be material if the Viet Namese drive out the French. If he joins then with a Communist China in full support of Soviet Russia, his present protestations will have been proven to be premature. Whether he will so join, or whether he will set up in Indo-China a democratic state (Asia style) with which the United States and Western Europe can have amicable relations depends not so much on Ho as it does on the actions of the United States and the European democracies. Certainly, just screaming "Communist" now at Ho Chi Minh will not change the course of events in Indo-China.

Uncle Ho, as he is affectionately called by his followers in a salutation that is common elsewhere in Asia for revered leaders, is the key figure of the revolutionary movement in Indo-China. To know him and to know the working of his mind is to understand the Viet Minh. In Indonesia there are a group of leaders who act and interact on each other so that it is difficult to say which is the more influential and which the more important in the Republic. In Indo-China, Ho Chi Minh is the commanding, the overwhelming presence.

If Ho Chi Minh is Nguyen Ai-Quoc, he began his revolutionary career at the age of twelve as a courier for a nationalist group in Central Annam, where he was born. His father was a minor official at the court of Bao Dai's father, and was one of the revolutionaries. When the movement was revealed and suppressed, the rest of the family were arrested and imprisoned. Ho Chi Minh, then nineteen, escaped and went to France. In Paris he worked at many things, but mostly for the independence of his own country. At the time of the Versailles Peace Conference in 1919, he was the recognized leader of the revolutionary movement of Indo-China. He drew up demands for independence that were presented to the treaty makers and brusquely put aside.

In those days Ho was a Socialist, a left-wing Socialist. When the French party split under the impetus of the Bolshevik Revolution in Russia, he joined with the dissenters to help found the French Communist party. He undoubtedly first knew there, and worked with, Chou En-lai and Chu Teh, two of the Chinese Communist leaders who were in France immediately after the war. He visited Germany, where the Communists were strong and active, and went to Moscow in 1923 as a delegate to the International Peasants' Congress.

After the Moscow meeting, Ho went to China and his whole life since has been in Asia. A facile language student, who now speaks half a dozen languages, including French, English, and Russian, Ho Chi Minh served in Canton for a time with the Kuomintang as a translator for the Russian Bolsheviks who were sent there by the Comintern to work with Dr. Sun Yat-sen, Chiang Kai-shek, Mao Tse-tung, and the other leaders of the Chinese Revolution.

With Canton and adjoining Hong Kong as his headquarters,

Uncle Ho—under his former name—directed the resistance to the French in Indo-China. Nguyen Ai-Quoc was a name whispered from one end of Indo-China to the other. He was reported here, there, and everywhere. Had he been a hundred men he could not have achieved half the feats that were credited to him by his awed followers, and the French Sûreté. He was both the leader of the revolution and its symbol.

Nor was his fame confined to Indo-China. He lived for a time in Bangkok and worked with Siamese revolutionaries. The back alleys of crowded Singapore knew him, too, and all the Chinatowns of Southeast Asia. He was never betrayed by his followers and, so far as is known, he was never arrested by the French. It was hardly conceivable that they ever had him in hand. He is too strikingly individual for them to have overlooked him. Hal Isaacs, an American newspaperman, recognized his face even in a poster in Hanoi after the war as the Annamite revolutionary he had known years before in China.

With the beginning of the full-scale war in the Pacific, in December, 1941, Ho Chi Minh went back to Tonkin to take active charge of the underground against first the French and the Japanese and then finally against the Japanese alone. Many American and British intelligence agents came to know and to respect him. With abandoned French stores, captured Japanese arms, and some American equipment that was dropped to him by plane, he waged a successful guerrilla war against communication lines and isolated garrisons in Indo-China. A full Japanese division could neither destroy his forces nor neutralize them. When the Japanese surrender came, he was ready, willing, and able to march into Hanoi and proclaim the Republic.

Ho is not physically impressive. He is small, even by Southeast Asian standards, some five feet one or two inches tall and weighing at the most 100 to 110 pounds. His scant hair is almost white, as is the wispy little goatee and moustache that he affects. His cheeks are sunken and he looks as if he were tubercular, which he once was. When Bob Trumbull, then Southeast Asia correspondent for the New York *Times*, and I saw him, he was in bed with what he said was a fever he had contracted while living in the hills with his guerrillas. He coughed occasionally and rubbed his hand across his forehead as though to brush away an ache.

There was no trace of an accent in his English as he greeted us from the middle of the enormous bed, in which he lay propped up on pillows, and offered us cakes and imported French champagne. (It was only eleven o'clock in the morning, but champagne is permissible in French etiquette at any time.) He did not drink himself. Nor did he smoke, although his yellowed fingers indicated he had. His doctor was very severe with him, he said smiling.

For ninety minutes he talked about the Viet Minh, about Viet Nam, about the French, about Americans and the great United States that he had never seen but for which, he said, he had much respect. He guaranteed Bob and me safe passage anywhere in territory controlled by the Viet Nam if we would show the American flag on our car or wear it on our clothing.

"The C.B.I. shoulder patch will do," he said. "That will be recognized." (That was the identifying insignia worn by American soldiers in the China-Burma-India theater.)

Ho had just come back at that time from Fontainebleau, where he had gone to work out the details of the accord he had signed with Jean Sainteny at Hanoi the previous March 6. When Admiral D'Argenlieu, in his absence, had set up a provisional government in Cochin China—whose allegiance was to have been determined in a plebiscite that has not yet been held—and called a conference at Dalat that included representatives from Viet Nam areas over which the March 6 accord had recognized the *de facto* control of the Republic, Ho and the French signed instead a *modus vivendi*, pending further negotiations. Under the *modus vivendi*, Viet Nam troops were limited to 10,000, to be under French command, French troops in Viet Nam territory were limited to 15,000, and there was to be joint patrol of shared cities, such as Hanoi, Haiphong, and Langsdon.

"My feeling toward the *modus vivendi*," Ho said, "is one of 'yes' and 'no.' 'Yes' because it was better than nothing. 'No' because it leaves the principal questions undecided. However, now that it's signed, we'll abide by it sincerely."

Conditions for peace, however, were not good, he continued. The French, he charged, had consistently violated the troop strength provisions of, first, the March 6 accord and, now, the *modus vivendi* (a charge that both Mr. Sainteny and Major General Jean Valluy, in Saigon, denied). The French even that week, he said, had reinforced their garrison at Tourane, a Central Annam port.

"We are ready to make peace," he declared. "We can assure the *status quo*. But they want a *fait accompli*. They are constantly trying to take more territory. When they send so many troops here, it isn't to make peace."

Ho said he never had been opposed to Indo-China remaining in a French Union. That was provided for in the March 6 accord. "We are willing to live as friends in the French house," he said, "but not in a French jail." The accord guaranteed priority of French citizens as advisers and technicians and experts on finance, business, and industry. That did not, however, give them a monopoly of such positions, nor were the French guaranteed their old monopolies in business and industry. What Viet Nam wanted and needed, he said, was foreign capital from other sources, advisers from the United States, technicians from United States mines and from United States factories to help Viet Nam industrialize and modernize what plants it had. Previous French investments were guaranteed.

For a long time, he said, the Viet Namese had hoped and had believed that the United States would insist on extension of the Atlantic Charter to cover Asia. They had hoped that a France that had known four years of brutal German occupation would recognize the yearning of the Viet Namese for independence and would grant it to them.

"We finally have come to believe that what we win we must win with our own resources," he continued. "Eventually we will win."

Outwardly, Viet Nam was a governing government. Viet Nam policemen regulated traffic in Hanoi. Governmental headquarters was guarded by smartly dressed, alert young soldiers. There was as much evidence of order by day as in the French-controlled cities, and questions were answered as explicitly and as frankly by Viet Namese officials as they were by French officials in Hanoi and in Saigon. Joint French and Viet Nam Army patrols moved through the city in trucks or armored cars. The cafés were open, and although the stores had few goods on their shelves, they had occasional customers; movement through the principal streets was orderly and unimpeded. The currency was Viet Namese, as were the stamps and the postal service.

The calm, however, was only on the surface (which was true also of Saigon). Deep ditches barred to vehicles all roads leading into the Viet Nam section of the city. At night rifle fire crackled through the streets. Some of it may have been at shadows, but the wounds suffered were real enough. French sentries stood their posts in pairs. A single Frenchman, out after dark, walked the middle of the street. In the shadows of the sidewalks, he stood a good possibility of receiving a dagger between his shoulder blades. Two weeks later, on December 19, when French soldiers began to fill in the trenches to open up the whole city, firing began that has not yet stopped and which will not halt, it is safe to predict, until the French either are driven out, until they make their peace with Ho Chi Minh or until, or if, Bao Dai weans away from Ho his present followers.

In the countryside, both before the final breakdown of the *modus vivendi* and since, according to all objective reports, the rule of Viet Nam was absolute. A strong French convoy might move from one town to another, but a single car dared not attempt it. A French force might seize a town, but its members were safe only by daylight and dared not move outside their guarded camp.

There was one French charge against the Viet Nam Government that hardly could be controverted: it did not live up to the terms of the truce. The Viet Namese blamed most of the incidents from their side as due to overzealous members of the Tu Ve, the "Self-Defense" organization of peasants. But it appeared too well organized for that. Mr. Sainteny, although crediting Ho Chi Minh himself with good intentions, was not so sure of the validity of the word of some of his ministers. Then, too, the French commissioner said, the Viet Nam radio and its printed literature was so violent against the French that it could hardly be expected that the irregulars would take seriously, and obey, orders not to fire on a Frenchman whenever they saw one. "The Ho Chi Minh Government is captive of its own propaganda," he said.

Wherever the fault lay for these armed clashes, there was no doubt in the mind of anyone—Frenchman, Annamite, or neutral observer—as to the hold Ho Chi Minh and the Viet Nam Government had on the people. Part of it may have been due to coercion of the great mass by the armed few, which was the French explanation. A better explanation is that no matter how unlettered a man may be, there still burns within him a desire to be free, a desire to be governed by his own people rather than by aliens, and especially aliens whose home is over ten thousand miles away. Given a free choice, most people would prefer, I believe, to be misgoverned by their own leaders than to be well governed by outsiders.

Which is not to say that the Viet Nam Government was incompetent. In 1946 the Ho Chi Minh leadership had two great accomplishments to its credit that no one denied. In one year of rule in the north it had alleviated famine conditions in Tonkin and Annam that, in the previous twelve months, had taken between 1,000,000 and 2,000,000 lives. (The first figure is the estimate of an American; the second is that of Ho Chi Minh himself.) The government had done this by halting exports of rice, by dike repair, and by a forced diversification of farming that had provided a substitute for the deficient rice supply. The French were not responsible for the famine. That had been caused by the Japanese, the Chinese occupying troops, and by nature. The first had converted many rice fields to castor-bean production and had requisitioned an overlarge portion of the rice that was left. The river Rouge, which flows out of the mountains past Hanoi to the sea at Haiphong, had broken through the crumbling levees—which the Japanese had not kept in repair during the war years—both in 1944 and 1945, flooding many rice paddies. When the Chinese troops from Yunan came in, they took what rice stores they wanted, not only to feed themselves and the troops that were transshipped through Tonkin for Manchuria and North China, but for export to their home province as well. By December, 1946, Ho Chi Minh boasted, there was no hunger in the areas controlled by Viet Nam.

The second great accomplishment of the Ho Chi Minh Government was that of educating the people. In one year, he boasted, 2,000,000 illiterate adults in Tonkin and Annam were taught to read and to write in the simplified "Quoc-Ngu" phonetic language that was codified by Father Alexandre de Rhodes, a French missionary, in the seventeenth century, but which the French had not attempted to teach. Inability to read was declared by Ho to be shameful. Such an adult education program as had not been attempted in Asia before was inaugurated. The simplicity of the language—which could be learned by an illiterate of average intelligence in two months—made the task easier than in Indonesia, where a similar program was instituted. As each adult learned his lessons, he was expected to become in turn a teacher.

No one walking casually around Hanoi would dispute Ho Chi Minh's figures of 2,000,000 persons taught in one year to read and to write. Typical was the watchman at the Standard Oil Company's headquarters in Hanoi. Going to the garage there one night with Don Gallagher, the Standard Oil representative, I saw the Annamite guard sitting with his wife under a dim electric light, teaching her to read. She in turn would teach their children and adult neighbors.

Ho Chi Minh may or may not be a Communist. The same may be true of other Viet Namese leaders. Their program is democratic. It has four main points. They are: (1) Feed the people. (That was done.) (2) Educate the people. (That is being rapidly accomplished.) (3) Give full freedom of speech, of worship, of assembly, of the press. (That is something difficult to evaluate.) (4) Establish friendly relations with all democratic states. (Cut off from the world, Viet Nam has had no opportunity to implement that one.)

What M. Jean Sainteny's views may be now, I do not know. He was one of the first Frenchmen wounded when fighting broke out in December, 1946. (A Viet Namese tossed a hand grenade through the window of his office.) On the night of December 5, 1946, at his dinner table in Hanoi, he told Bob Trumbull and me, "I believe Ho Chi Minh to be a sincere patriot."

PART IV. FRANCE IN THE PACIFIC

CHAPTER 3. *Admiral D'Argenlieu and the Colonials*

The women of Indo-China are tiny, fine-boned, and thinly fleshed. They go shopping in midafternoon in Saigon dressed in white-silk trousers over which they wear beautifully colored and embroidered long gowns such as one sees in Shanghai or Peiping. Their black hair is beautifully done and their painted toenails show through their openwork sandals. It was they, you believe, and not the Burmese of whom Kipling must have been thinking when he wrote, in "Mandalay," that there's "a neater, sweeter maiden in a cleaner, greener land!"

On an afternoon in mid-December, 1946, one of these lovely doll-like women clenched a fist that was no larger than a baby's and told an American friend, "If the admiral returns, blood will flow." Two days later, it was announced from Paris that Rear Admiral Thierry D'Argenlieu, French high commissioner for the Pacific and governor-general of Indo-China, who had been in Paris for consultations with the government, was returning to Saigon to resume his posts. Two days later the *modus vivendi* Ho Chi Minh and the French had signed at Fontainebleau in October was torn to shreds by grenade fragments and bullets in Hanoi, and one of the most vicious and merciless colonial wars in history was again in full swing.

No one Frenchman probably should be blamed for what has gone on in Indo-China since 1945. But it is a fact that history is written by men and not events alone and that dominant personalities often have changed its course. If a villian of the piece is needed, the admiral will do for Indo-China.

Admiral D'Argenlieu is one of the oddities of colonial government in Asia. Until the fall of France in 1940, he was a Carmelite monk, head of that Catholic order in France. He escaped from the Nazis and joined De Gaulle in London. Before joining the Carmelites he had been in the French Navy, so De Gaulle named him a rear admiral in the Free French Navy and, with the British Government's assent, sent him to the Pacific in an effort to save from the men of Vichy the off-shore possessions of the French—New Caledonia, the New Hebrides, and the various smaller island groups to the eastward. New Caledonia is the seat of this Pacific empire.

United States Navy and Army officers became acquainted with the admiral there in the spring of 1942, when New Caledonia, whose capital and seaport is Nouméa, and the New Hebrides were occupied successively in preparation for the attack on Guadalcanal and the start of the long, island-road to Tokyo Bay. The French colonials in New Caledonia were in almost open revolt against Admiral D'Argenlieu when the Americans moved in. He had come out from London clothed in an overpowering dignity which considerably irked his compatriots. He requisitioned the best houses and the best cars for himself and his staff. He had a section of the best bathing beach roped off for himself. When he and his unofficial hostess, Madame Galsworthy, French-born wife of an English liaison aide of his, wanted to go swimming, the admiral sent word ahead to have the beach cleared.

Several of the leading citizens of Nouméa became so enraged that they refused to obey his orders. He had them arrested and shipped off to exile on the adjoining small Isle of Pines. The admiral gave the impression that it was a Vichy-inspired revolt. During negotiations for their return, the admiral went to the home of one of the negotiators for the week end. The story is that when he visited one of the outbuildings, his host locked him in and refused to unlock the door until he had promised to bring back the exiles and deal with them on a basis of equality.

It was this strutting little man with whom American military officials, who were fighting a bitter war on a shoestring, had to deal when they moved in, in March, 1942, and started building up Nouméa as one of the main South Pacific bases. After some futile efforts at cooperation they finally decided it was easier to just go ahead and do what was necessary and largely ignore the admiral. This they did. Some Frenchmen complained that it would have been better had the Japanese come, which was a very real fear that spring of 1942, instead of the Americans; but since they were dependent on the United States Navy for practically everything from gasoline to food, they said these things only privately.

That was the kind of an administrator, however, who was sent to Indo-China to restore French rule there after the Japanese had been beaten in the Pacific, with, it should be added, no help from the French in Indo-China and little from those scattered elsewhere around the Pacific on their island paradises.

Whether Admiral D'Argenlieu was acting under orders from Paris or improvising on the spot, it was he who quite effectively sabotaged the March 6, 1946, accord that M. Sainteny and Ho Chi Minh signed in Hanoi and which never was carried out by the French. One of its provisions was that a plebiscite be held in Cochin China to decide whether it would join Viet Nam or remain an independent state in an Indo-China Federation within a French Union. The admiral said no plebiscite could be held until "order is restored." Then he set up a provisional government, with an Assembly appointed half by the chiefs and half by French business interests in Indo-China. The Assembly, in turn, named the President. The first one committed suicide, saying he could not stand the disapproval of his people.

The Cochin China Provisional Government was obviously under the domination of the French. French "advisers" ran the show in Saigon much as United States Army "advisers" did in Korea. French judges interpreted the law and the evidence. The principal French "adviser" had a large, fan-cooled office and his own chauffeured motor car. The provisional President had a desk in a bare office and went to lunch in a downtown café in a hired rickshaw. The provisional government was a legal fiction that fooled no one, least of all those Indo-Chinese who took a shame-faced part in the farce.

When Admiral D'Argenlieu was called back to his priestly duties by the Vatican in early 1947, the course of events were so frozen in Indo-China that little change was possible without French "loss of face," a prideful disease that has long been attributed to all Asiatics by the white man but from which the white man suffers much more than his brown- or yellow-skinned counterpart.

All the Frenchmen in Indo-China did not think as did Admiral D'Argenlieu and others of the colonial group who came over from Oceania with him or out of their short internment by the Japanese to attempt to set up shop in the same old prewar colonial style. Jean Sainteny in Hanoi apparently had the respect of the Viet Namese. Major General Jean Valluy, the French commander in chief in the Pacific in 1946 and 1947, was said by the Viet Namese to be friendly to them, conscious of their aspirations, and to frown on the excesses of the Sûreté and of his own troops. Had they had those two only to deal with, said members of Ho Chi Minh's government and some Viet Minh leaders Bob Trumbull and I met in Saigon, peace would have been maintained and a friendly relationship with France in a French Union would have been established.

Most of the French newspapermen in Saigon were bitter against the colonial overlords. Many of the newspapermen were former resistance fighters in metropolitan France who had come out to Indo-China after the war to start life anew. Some of them had been imprisoned and tortured by the Germans. They knew what it was to suffer for one's country and for freedom. When there was a threat that Admiral D'Argenlieu would close some of the press, the staffs of sixteen of the eighteen French papers in Saigon formed a press union and told the admiral that if one was closed, all would cease printing.

These French newspapermen—worthy inheritors of the ideals of the First Republic—established contact with the Viet Minh and printed from time to time reports of the terrible reprisals inflicted by the French troops on villages near which convoys, bringing in rice or products from the French-owned estates, had been attacked. Every day or so one or more of the papers would carry a report such as this: "Four days ago a patrol of the Army descended on the village of Viet Minh, near which a convoy was ambushed four days previously. Two of the eighteen men of the village were summarily executed. The other sixteen were taken to Saigon. No word has been received from them since. The village was burned." There have been a hundred Lidice's in Indo-China, not just one.

The French newspapermen established a club, where good food was served at cost and which was an oasis of democracy in a desert of colonialism. When one of the more outspoken of the papers was dispossessed from its quarters by the admiral on the pretext that the space was needed for a government department, its staff set up shop in the club and kept on printing their thinly disguised criticism of the admiral's administration. The French information chief kept a man "on duty" in the club at all times. "The Spy," the newspapermen called him. He generally sat alone, conspicuously ignored by the members. Bob and I met there one day a Viet Namese courier from Ho Chi Minh's headquarters to whom we were introduced by two of the French reporters.

Although there was no open censorship of foreign correspondents' dispatches, those of the French reporters to Paris were cut, withheld, or delayed so long they lost their value, we were told. "The people of France don't know what is going on down here," one of them said bitterly. "If they did, they wouldn't stand for it." There had been talk for some time at the club of setting up a clandestine radio station to report directly to Paris, but the plan never was carried through. For one thing it was dangerous. Several of the younger newspapermen were French Army reservists. If any of them got too far out of line, the admiral saw to it they were called back to France to do their army service.

A faith that had the people of France known what was happening in Indo-China they would have ordered a change was one that was held not alone by some of the Frenchmen in Saigon. There was a Dr. ——— (whom I dare not better identify) to whom Bob and

I were introduced one afternoon during our stay in Saigon. He had been educated in France but had returned to Indo-China to work with his own people. He married on his return and in time became the father of two sons. He sent both to Paris to school.

When the war came, one of the sons still was in France. He joined the resistance, was finally captured by the Germans, and died under torture without betraying his group. The other son was back in Indo-China. With the end of the war he joined Viet Minh and was named a member of the Executive Committee of Viet Minh in Cochin China. He was picked up one day by the Sûreté. He "died" in prison. The body was returned to his parents in a sealed coffin.

As the aging doctor told us these things, he pointed to a table on which stood pictures of the two boys. One died for France, the other in French hands. "But I still believe," said the doctor, tears running down his face as he spoke, "that the French people I know and love do not approve of these things, that some day they will grant us the freedom we want and which Frenchmen always have treasured for themselves." As I listened, I wondered what France could buy with the piasters they could get from a subservient Indo-China that was one-half as precious as what they have lost there.

Part of the doctor's faith in France had been restored by a little French soldier who had come to his house in Saigon one day not long before Bob and I met him. This boy was a friend of his son, the one who had been killed by the Germans. They had been in prison together. The boy was delighted when his unit was ordered to French Indo-China. He wanted to see his friend's parents to tell them how bravely their son had died for France. Before he could get leave to search them out after the arrival of his unit in Saigon, he was sent out with a patrol to destroy a village that was under suspicion as a Viet Minh base. The village was a typical one of straw-thatched huts set within a wall of thorn trees. The French patrol was deployed around the village and ordered to fire incendiary bullets into the huts. Machine guns had been set up to cover the openings in the thorn hedge; and as the people attempted to escape, they were shot down. The young soldier was reported as having fired his rifle in the air. When he had served his term of imprisonment, he sought out the doctor and asked him to put him in touch with the Viet Minh. He wanted to desert and join them to fight now against France as he once had risked his life for her against the Germans. The doctor did not say what he, or the boy, had done. If he deserted, he was only one of hundreds who did, including many of the German members of the French Foreign Legion, who had been recruited out of prisoner-of-war camps in 1945 and 1946 and sent out in French uniforms to shoot down people who were seeking their freedom, the right to decide their own destiny.

In late 1946 it was said in Saigon that there were 10,000 Foreign Legionnaires in Indo-China and that of those, 6,000 were Germans. General Valluy, when asked about it, denied there were that many but he did not give any alternative figure. An American in Hanoi one night heard some of the German-speaking Legionnaires in a café singing the hymn of Hitler and the Nazis, the "Horst Wessel" song. Three of them went one night to the room of an American officer with a German name and asked him to help them escape the Legion and Indo-China. They wanted to go to the United States.

Bitter, brutal, disillusioned with Hitler but unrepentant, these German Legionnaires were blamed by some Frenchmen for the excesses practiced against the Viet Namese. Maybe. Frenchmen, too, blamed the Viet Namese for beginning the campaign of atrocities. Perhaps that, too, is true. There was little doubt that atrocities were committed on both sides. Bodies of French soldiers were found mutilated. Few captives were taken in skirmishes by either side. Two former Germans in the Foreign Legion arrived in Bangkok, Siam, while I was there in January, 1947. They said they were the only survivors of a patrol of fifty men that had been ambushed. They were able to identify themselves to the Viet Nam soldiers as Germans and were taken to the Siamese border and released. All others of their patrol were killed, even those who attempted to surrender.

An American officer who met War Minister Giap of the Viet Nam Government in 1946 urged on him that the Viet Nam Army live up fully to the Geneva Convention governing warfare and treatment of prisoners. Early in 1947 Mr. Giap broadcast an announcement that he had issued such an order. Whether it was obeyed, whether the public promise was kept, I do not know.

When the accord of March 6, 1946, was signed between France and Viet Nam, it was greeted everywhere as a fair solution of the colonial problem. The Dutch in Indonesia based the Linggadjati Agreement on it. The accord was never implemented. For that the French were to blame. The price has been a colonial war that cost Paris at least $700,000,000, probably more, during 1947 and 1948, at which time the French military position in Indo-China was worsening every day. No one who knew the country held any hope that Bao Dai could rally more than a token support as the "democratic" head of an independent Indo-China. Help was on the way for Ho Chi Minh. He had asked for it from the United States and from the United Nations and he had been ignored. A Communist-dominated government in China undoubtedly would give a different answer. In early 1949 time seemed to be running out on France.

PART V. BRITAIN IN THE PACIFIC

CHAPTER 1. *The Fijis and Other Islands*

An old Norwegian freighter limped out of the harbor of Suva, the capital city of the Fiji Islands and seat of Britain's Pacific Islands Government, on a morning in April, 1943, and turned her nose north and east toward San Francisco. A young Australian mining engineer, enroute to a new assignment in Canada, with somewhat misty eyes watched the beautiful coast of Viti Levu fade away into only a green line where sea and sky met.

"I am so sorry to leave," he said. "I shall never know finer people than these."

He did not mean the 6,000 Europeans, the Eurasians, the few Chinese, or the other outlanders who live in the Fiji Islands. Certainly he did not mean the 125,000 Indians, whose forefathers had come to the Fijis as indentured labor and had remained to multiply until they were the largest ethnic and national group. He meant the estimated 120,000 dark-skinned, bushy-haired original inhabitants who, until the last few years, had seemed on their way to extinction or at best to life as a minority group in the islands of their ancestors.

Other white men who have gone to the Fijis and other islands of the South Seas to patronize and to exploit and who have remained to love and to respect the South Pacific peoples may differ with the Australian. Each has his own favorite. Mine are the Polynesians. But there was no doubting the depth of emotion or the sincerity of my young Australian friend about the Fijians. His opinion was confirmed by my own brief observation of them and acquaintanceship with them.

Against every sort of pressure, including the impact of two world wars, the peoples of the South Pacific have maintained their integrity, their dignity, and even some of their old ways of life. And nowhere is this more true than in the islands that form the British Empire in the South Seas—the Fijis, the Gilbert and Ellice islands, the Solomons, the New Hebrides, Pitcairn, and the Tongans. It diminishes to the westward, where Melanesia and Micronesia overlap and where there never had been a very high degree of culture or of dignity. Today these wards of the king can look forward to an even happier future than has been their past, for the last three hundred years at least. And British overlordship has not been an unmixed evil. It has its good points.

Exploitation really is the wrong word to use in describing British empire building in the South Seas. Except for the Fijis, most of the islands are an economic liability. They were acquired more by accident than by design, and their chief values were as coaling stations or as producers of scarce raw materials that were needed in Europe, such as copra, from which are extracted the oils for soap making.

Most of the British South Sea Islands, which are ruled by a British high commissioner from Suva, lie between the Tropic of Capricorn and the Equator. There are hundreds of them, of coral or volcanic formation, but with a total population of only about 500,000. Of these an estimated 275,000 live in the Fijis, 36,000 in the Gilbert and Ellice islands, 100,000 in the Solomons, 45,000 in the Tongans, and 50,000 in the New Hebrides, which is ruled jointly by Britain and France under what is called a Condominium (pronounced "pandemonium" by the cynical).

All became familiar to Americans during the war, by name if nothing else. The Fijis and the Tongan islands were early air and naval bases. The New Hebrides were advance bases for the Guadalcanal campaign and other operations in the Solomons. The Gilbert and Ellice islands were air bases for the attack on the Marshalls, Tarawa, in the Gilberts, being the scene of one of the United States Marines' most bitter and costly island operations. The Solomons, of course, were where were won the first American victories in 1942 and 1943.

The most advanced, politically, economically, and culturally, of the islands over which flies the British flag, are the Fijis and the Tongans. The Fijis are a colony; the Tongans are a kingdom under British protection. Both had a long history of tribal government—not always peaceful—and a high culture before the advent of the British, or any other white men in the Pacific. Both came under the British flag during the empire-building days of the nineteenth century.

The Fijis have been a British possession since 1874. In that year King Thakombau, head of the most powerful tribe, pledged allegiance to Queen Victoria after having been several times rebuffed in that effort. Ten years previously he had tried to interest President Lincoln in accepting such a pledge in return for cancellation of a $45,000 claim made against him by American residents. Lincoln was busy with the Civil War and did not even answer his petition.

The Fijis have been among the most orderly and peaceful of Britain's subjects since that time. For which much thanks must go to the Christian missionaries, who first began working in the islands in 1830. These missionaries apparently were of a high caliber. In two generations they had transformed the Fijis from a warlike people of relatively uncivilized ways to a sober, peacefully inclined race, whose leaders have been educated in New Zealand, Australia, and England and have gone back to help their people work and educate themselves toward self-government.

Most influential of these British-educated Fijians is Ratu Sir Joseva Lalabalavu Vanaaliali Sukuna, a collateral descendant of Thakombau and Secretary for Fijian Affairs in the Fiji Government. Before that, he was native land commissioner. Ratu Sukuna is one of the most impressive men I ever have met. He was a student at Oxford in 1914 when the First World War began. He offered his services to the British, but there was no place for a black man, except in a stevedoring job or in a native regiment, so he went across the Channel and enlisted in the French Foreign Legion. In two years he had acquired every French decoration, including the Medal Militaire—the highest decoration. The British then called him back and commissioned him to raise a regiment of his fellows in the Fijis. He did, but they spent the rest of the war in menial tasks.

Returning to London after the war, Ratu Sukuna—or Sir Lala, as he may now be called since being knighted—took his examinations as a barrister and was admitted to the Middle Temple. He returned then to his own land and was appointed native land commissioner; no Fijian land could be sold or leased without his permission.

When the Second World War began, he again offered his services to his king. He was made a major and given the task of raising a Fijian defense force, which he did by calling a council of chiefs and assigning quotas to each village. A force of four thousand men was raised, commanded by New Zealanders. For many months after the Japanese attack they did only guard duty, stevedoring at Suva, and menial tasks around the United States camps and air bases that were established. Finally the stupidity of the American and Allied commands was broken down—largely through the fine scouting work done by a group of thirty who were taken as a trial to Guadalcanal—and on Bougainville a battalion of them wrote one of the bravest chapters of Pacific War history.

Ratu Sukuna is a good prototype of the Fijian—six feet tall and beautifully proportioned, with the finely developed legs that have come from centuries of going places afoot. His classical schooling in New Zealand and in England have given him a command of English that his white contemporaries envy; even his short memorandums have a felicity of phrase that is a delight. He is equally at home in the ceremonial dress of a Fiji chief or clothes from London. Generally he wears an English jacket, the South Seas wraparound, knee-length skirt which is called a lava lava in the Fijis, and open leather sandals.

A New Zealand officer who had worked with Ratu Sukuna and knew his capabilities was speaking of him one night at the other end of a dinner table in Suva during the war.

"If he said the word," this officer said, "every white man in the Fijis would wake up tomorrow morning with his throat cut."

Ratu Sukuna never gave the word, and he never will. Like Sutan Sjahrir, of Indonesia, and other of the more intelligent leaders of the South Seas and Southeast Asia, Ratu Sukuna believes there is no good reason why the white man, the black, the yellow, and the brown cannot live and work together for their mutual benefit. The "Jim Crowism" to which he was subjected in the United States several years ago and the indifferent way in which the offer of his services in two wars was accepted by the British could have embittered him, as similar slights have Paul Robeson and other men of color. But Ratu Sukuna apparently has met enough white men to know that all of them do not believe the color of a man's skin is an index of his worth.

The Fijis two principal exports are sugar and gold, the profits of which both largely are monopolized by white men. The imported Indians crop the sugar for white planters and Ted Theodore, an Australian, owns the principal gold mine. The Fijians, however, are not jealous of the profits. Which requires some explaining.

The Fijians, like most of the island peoples of the Pacific, have for centuries lived an easy-going communal life. Tropic fruits and roots were theirs for little effort, and the sea provided the fish and the sea growths, rich with iodine, to complete their diet. The warm climate made clothing a matter of secondary importance. To this day they cannot understand the white man's mad rush through the years accumulating things he cannot possibly use in his lifetime and will have no use for after that. A South Sea islander would understand perfectly Grandpa Vanderhof, the principal character of the Kaufman-Hart play *You Can't Take It with You,* that was so popular on the New York stage a few years ago. The Fijian prefers to work only as much as is necessary, play when he feels like it, and laugh a lot. If he dies, he knows his neighbors will take care of his family.

Somewhere between that traditional indolence (or just common sense) of the island people and the push and drive, the Chamber of Commerce attitude, of the white intruder may lie a golden mean. It is such a mean that leaders like Ratu Sukuna and Queen Salote, of Tonga, are seeking. Whether they like it or not, the island peoples must adapt themselves, at least in part, to Western ways. There is no turning the clock back. Their old cup has been broken and there is no chance of patching it together again. A new one must be shaped and hardened if they are to survive.

And it is a question of survival. The white man brought to them his diseases as well as clothing and trinkets and alarm clocks. An influenza epidemic during the First World War killed the island peoples by the thousands. It is one reason that the Fijians today are numerically inferior to the Indians.

The Indian population is the major Fiji problem, both for the Fijians and for the British administrators. Some of them have lived in the Fijis so long they have no desire to return to their native India. Yet they are treated as inferiors, denied a voice in the government of the islands, and barred from buying land and really settling down to make the Fijis their permanent home. They were a problem before the war and are undoubtedly a much greater one now, with India a free country. Although brought to the Fijis as laborers, they have branched out into many other activities, as artisans and shopkeepers. With their off-island industry they could very well become the predominant race economically as they already are numerically.

The Kingdom of Tonga is one of the ideal arrangements worked out between the island peoples and the white man. It is a constitutional monarchy under British protection. Like the Fijians the Tongans are magnificent physical specimens, their queen being six feet six inches in height and proportioned accordingly. They have no problem of race, since there never has been an importation of labor to their islands. The only outlanders among their 45,000 people are some 250 Europeans and 750 others of mixed blood.

The present Tongan dynasty traces its line back over one thousand years, to before the Normans conquered England. Queen Salote ascended the throne in 1918 on the death of her father, King George Tubou. Educated in New Zealand, she governs her kingdom with a Legislative Assembly and the aid of a British adviser. And she governs it well. The Tongan Islands have an export balance of almost 50 per cent; in 1947 imports totaled $1,500,000 and exports, largely copra, were worth $3,000,000.

Queen Salote, and her father before her, have drawn in their kingdom a good balance between their own and the white civilizations. They established agricultural schools to teach their people better ways of growing crops, but in the same schools they teach also the old Tongan crafts, of which the making of tapa cloth (a beautifully dyed cloth made of tree bark) is the best example.

During the war Queen Salote sent her people back into the hills to their old villages when the United States moved in to make Nukualofa, on the island of Tongatabu, a big air and naval base. The war years did not lead to the degradation of the native peoples there as it did in some other places. She also has been a proponent of better medical care, being the first supporter of the idea of a medical school in the Fijis, where selected students from many South Sea islands are given a two-year course in hygiene, sanitation, and preventive medicine and then sent back home to help make of the South Sea Islands a healthier and better place for the native.

Two years ago there was formed a South Pacific Commission, composed of official representatives of Australia, France, the Netherlands, New Zealand, the United Kingdom, and the United States. Offices have been established at Nouméa, on New Caledonia, and a working staff set up.

The avowed aim of the commission is to improve the health, the economy, and to promote the general welfare of the people of the South Pacific Islands. How fast this can be done is problematical.

The commission staff is small and funds are limited. But at least a start has been made. It can do no harm for the West to study the problems and attempt to understand them. It might do a great deal of good. As the people of Fiji and the Tongan Islands have proved, the South Pacific islander has capable leaders among his own people if they are given an education and an opportunity.

PART V. BRITAIN IN THE PACIFIC

CHAPTER 2. *Singapore and Malaya*

Three elements, one indigenous and two imported, have combined to make Singapore and the Malay Peninsula important assets of the British Empire. The one indigenous element is the tin that threads through the subsurface of her jungle-clothed mountain ranges. The two imported are the rubber plants, that were sneaked out of Brazil, developed at the Royal Botanical Gardens at Kew and then shipped to Malaya, and the vision of Sir Stamford Raffles, who got Britain to trade British claims in Sumatra for Dutch claims in Singapore and Malaya.

The tin and the rubber have been for over half a century Malaya's two most important exports. They still are. Sumatra is still a sparsely settled, although oil-rich, Dutch possession; Singapore has been for over a hundred years the British-held economic gateway to the Far East, through whose great port passes commerce more valuable to Britain than the black gold from the Sumatran oil wells.

The three most important elements of the Malayan economy—tin, rubber, and commerce—have brought the Malayans prosperity but also great problems.

Like most Southeast Asia and South Pacific peoples, the Malays are a soft-spoken but proud race who prize their independence and peace of mind above riches. They were reluctant to enter the tin mines and Chinese laborers were imported to work them. They objected likewise to work on the big rubber plantations, so Indians were imported to tap the trees and drain off the sticky substance that helped put the world on wheels—automobile wheels, that is. Their nature making them poor businessmen, they soon found themselves crowded out of the great commercial city of Singapore.

Like the Fijians, the Malayans are a minority race now in their own country, totaling an estimated 2,200,000 of Singapore's and Malaya's more than 5,000,000. The Chinese, over half of whom are concentrated in Singapore, total almost as many, and the Indians are estimated to number 750,000. The Europeans, exclusive of British armed forces, total only 20,000.

Singapore and Malaya—which are separated politically now, as they always have been physically by the Strait of Johore—are two of five British-controlled areas that are governed out of Singapore by a British commissioner-general. The others are British North Borneo, which became a Crown Colony in 1946, Sarawak, for many years a State ruled by the British Brookes family but which also became a Crown Colony by cession in 1946, and Brunei, a British protectorate. All are on the big island of Borneo that lies to the southeast of the Malay Peninsula, across the South China Sea; the remainder of Borneo is under Dutch rule. Sarawak is the most densely populated of the three, with an estimated total of 500,000 inhabitants. Brunei has 30,000 and North Borneo about 250,000. Rubber is the chief export of North Borneo, and rubber and oil of the other two. The people are largely Moslem in religion and peacefully inclined. Relative to Malaya and Singapore, they are not very important either politically or economically.

There have been some evidences since the war, though, of a stirring of nationalism even there, stimulated by the active revolt against colonialism in the Dutch East Indies which has resulted in formation of the United States of Indonesia. The now independent states in Dutch Borneo are looking toward their northern cousins and undoubtedly will stimulate discussion there of eventual union. At the Round Table Conference at The Hague in August and September, 1949, where the U.S. of I. was finally hammered into shape, the Indonesians were talking privately of eventual incorporation in their independent country of not only Sarawak, Brunei, and

British Borneo but of Singapore and Malaya as well. That, however, seems to be something considerably in the future.

The island of Singapore and the Malay Peninsula above it stretch for 500 miles southwest from Siam to the Equator and the Strait of Malacca. Singapore is a flat island with an area of less than 200 square miles on which live more than 1,000,000 people. The peninsula itself is dominated by two parallel mountain ranges, with peaks of 5,000 to 7,000 feet, that slope down sharply to a narrow coastal plain. The whole is densely covered by rain forests. Because of its proximity to the Equator, Malaya has only one season, although there are some periods of the year when there is less rainfall than others, the wetter season coming during what is the winter season in the northern latitudes when the wet monsoon is blowing up from Antarctica.

Malaya is not the forbidding land that it is so often painted, as Colonel F. Spencer Chapman, one of the leaders of the British-organized underground in Malaya against the Japanese, so brilliantly proved in his book of war adventures entitled *The Jungle Is Neutral.* The British, in their more than fifty years of political control of the country, largely eliminated malaria. Exploitation of the tin mines and importation of the rubber plants made Singapore and Malaya relatively prosperous areas of Asia before the war. Singapore has exceeded prewar totals of tonnage as a port; and although decreased tin and rubber purchases by the United States (because substitutes had been found for both) put a severe strain on Malayan economy, it appears probable that good markets for both rubber and tin eventually will be found again.

Politically, the condition has been more stable in Malaya—where there was really more real reason for instability—than it has been in either bordering French Indo-China or in Indonesia. This is because the British were far wiser in their handling of the problem of resurgent nationalism than were either of their fellow European colonial powers, the Dutch and the French.

Under the able leadership of Lord Killearn and Malcolm Mac-

Donald, son of England's late Labor Prime Minister, the British negotiated with the people of Malaya and of Singapore a charter of government that kept both within the British Empire—and by choice, not by coercion. When the first pact of federation negotiated with the sultans brought protests from the nationalists that their aspirations had not been met, the British answer was to reopen the talks and work out an agreement more agreeable to them.

Like all compromises, it was not entirely satisfactory to anyone. It split off Singapore from the peninsula politically, because otherwise the Malayan Union would have been Chinese instead of Malayan. It therefore did not please the Chinese, who have the biggest economic stake in the country. But it did provide for a common citizenship, opening that door to Malay's two nonindigenous races—the Chinese and the Indians. It protected, in the meantime, the interests of the Malays in their own land.

Control of the country still remains in British hands; the high commissioner still has veto power over much legislation. But, by providing for an elected assembly, the Malayan agreement provided a start toward that self-government which is the aspiration of all people. Eventually Singapore and the peninsula must be reunited. Nothing else makes either political or economic sense. But to do that now would cause greater cleavages than exist between the various ethnic groups. The best chance for an orderly progression to self-government is for an amalgam of the three races—Malay, Chinese, Indian. If they remain compartmented as today, and the Chinese continue to propagate as rapidly as they have in the past, then Malaya becomes either a Chinese-dominated country or there may develop communal warfare more disastrous than that in India in 1947. Nowhere else have the Chinese been assimilated, but just because something has not happened before is not a valid reason for supposing that it can never happen.

It is a precarious balance that is being maintained in Malaya, with some strange alliances that go against nature. The Malays cling to the British because they see in them their best hope to remain politically dominant in their own country. The wealthier Chinese are more fearful of what the Communist minority within their own community might do to them were it not for British protection than they are of being ruled by a Malayan minority or of being restricted politically to the small island of Singapore.

What course communism takes in China may determine what happens in Malaya, where there has been a Communist party since 1920. Should the Chinese Communists prove to be more nationalist than communist, they might rally to their side most of the Chinese scattered through Southeast Asia. A Titoesque government in Peiping or Nanking, that proved itself independent of Moscow and allowed some individual enterprise, would find strong support among the "Overseas" Chinese, as they call themselves, in Singapore, Malaya, and all through Southeast Asia.

It is these strong emotional ties with home, which are so important among the Chinese, that make the question of communism in Southeast Asia so incalculable a factor. The record of the Chinese community in Malaya is a good example of what has happened elsewhere. It has been particularly important in Singapore and Malaya because of the dominant position of the Chinese in the country.

When Dr. Sun Yat-sen began his revolution against the Manchus in China, he looked overseas for his financial support. As the revolution began to succeed in the 1920's, culminating in the Northern Expedition and the capture of the Yangtze River Valley, nationalism blossomed everywhere among the Overseas Chinese. And nowhere more verdantly than in Malaya. Then came Chiang-Kai-shek's purge of the Communists from the Kuomintang in 1927. The Overseas Chinese split, as did the Chinese in China. The Malayan Communist party, organized by Ho Chi Minh, the Indo-Chinese leader when he was Comintern agent for Southeast Asia, went underground. The Kuomintang, or K.M.T., as it is generally known, was dominant in Singapore and the Malayan towns and as ruthless as was Chiang.

Until the Japanese attack on North China in 1937, the Malayan Communist party remained an unimportant element in the life of

Singapore and Malaya. The rapprochement between Chiang and the Chinese Communists at Sian and hatred of the Japanese invader again made the Overseas Chinese a united people. The Communists took quick advantage of it. They became active in the anti-Japanese organization, known as the Anti-Enemy-Backing-Up-Society, and in a short time had their leaders in many of the important posts.

Although the ostensible purpose of the organization was to collect money for the fight against the Japanese, the Communists did not, of course, lose the opportunity in meetings to teach communist doctrine. They had, in the meantime, broadened the base of the Communist party in Malaya to take in what Malayans and Indians they could convert to Marxism.

The Malayan Communist party gave its first real show of strength in the fall of 1939 at the start of the war, after Moscow and Berlin had signed their pact that permitted Hitler to attack Poland. The Anti-Enemy-Backing-Up-Society that had branches all over Malaya became anti-British. There were mass demonstrations and strikes all over Malaya and finally a general strike that almost paralyzed the British war effort in Malaya for several months.

When Hitler turned on his erstwhile ally and attacked Russia in 1941, the Malayan Communist line did an abrupt about-face, of course, as did the party line everywhere. The imperialist war suddenly became one of the people's democracies. Churchill's picture went up in the meeting halls alongside that of Stalin. Then came the Japanese attack.

The only organized group in Malaya on which could be built any sort of an underground organization to send out information and to sabotage Japanese installations was the Malayan Communist party. Centuries of Dutch and British rule had changed the Malayas from a once warlike, pirating race to the most peacefully inclined in Southeast Asia. They had little love for the Japanese, but not much for the British, either. Those who were recruited by the British did well, but there were few of them and the effort was begun too late. Mostly the Malays remained neutral and suffered the fate of all such—persecution by both sides.

All through the war the Chinese Communists in Malaya provided the core of what organized resistance there was to the Japanese. They established camps in the hills, with the aid of a few British, from which to raid Japanese railway lines and ammunition dumps and to pin down Japanese troops. It is this organization, which was armed by the British in the late days of the war, which has caused all the trouble in Malaya since. Their campaign of terrorism, begun in 1947, which was directed against their non-Communist Chinese brethren as well as against British planters and noncooperating Malays, raised the whole peninsula against them, however, and the British were able largely to track them down and break the back of their movement. As in Indonesia, they struck too soon and with too little.

Whether Malaya ever again will become one of the more lustrous jewels in the crown of empire depends on many factors that are beyond the control of the British: revival of rubber and tin markets, Malayan progress toward self-government, the birth rate (which is still running strongly for the Chinese). Mostly it depends on the imponderables of racial amalgamation, at least on the political level, with the three great ethnic groups of Singapore and Malaya learning to think of themselves as common citizens of one country. That would be a miracle that could radically change the face of Asia. It is a miracle for which some believe there already is a precedent, at least in part, in the Hawaiian Islands under the American flag.

PART VI. THE EAST INDIES

CHAPTER 1. *The United States of Indonesia*

It took four and one-half years of intermittent fighting, the loss of an estimated 100,000 Dutch and Indonesian lives, and millions of dollars of destruction and millions more of trade losses to create the United States of Indonesia. Measured against the duration of other revolutions of peoples seeking their freedom, the time does not seem long. The Indonesians probably do not count the price too high. The tragedy is that all the fighting, all the losses were unnecessary.

Until July 20, 1947, it appeared that the always painful transition from colonialism to independence in the East Indies was to be made peacefully. There had been some fighting when the British landed at Batavia and other ports in September, 1945, after the Japanese capitulation and the proclamation by the Indonesian nationalists of the Republic of Indonesia. There had been even more when the Dutch troops began to arrive. But at the hill town of Linggadjati, near Cheribon, Java, on November 15, 1946, the Dutch and the Republicans had signed an agreement that was accepted as a good and clear blueprint for a peaceful compromise of conflicting Dutch claims and Indonesian aspirations. It called for the formation of a United States of Indonesia, of which the Republic would comprise the islands of Java, Sumatra, and Madoera, where lived 50,000,000 of Indonesia's population of 72,000,000. The other states were to be Borneo and East Indonesia. The United States of Indonesia would be part of the Netherlands Union of which metropolitan Netherlands would be another part and the Dutch possessions in the West

Indies—Curaçao, Aruba, and Surinam—a third, all under the Crown of Orange.

On July 20, 1947, however, the Dutch began what they called a "police action" and what most of the rest of the world judged a full-scale military campaign, to break the strength of the Republic and impose their own solution. It was one of the great mistakes of history. Armed with modern British and American equipment, the 120,000 Dutch troops, with complete control of the air and all sea approaches, quickly reached their assigned objectives, penned the Republic into the least productive part of the island of Java and the hill country of Sumatra, and began the imposition of law and order in the seized territories. The battle was won. The war was lost.

The first "police action" so outraged public opinion in most of the world that the Dutch, to their great surprise, found themselves boycotted in India and Australia, cited to the United Nations as a menace to world peace, and called before the Security Council to justify their course.

When a United Nations Commission finally negotiated a new agreement between the Dutch and the Republic in January, 1948, which was signed aboard the American attack transport U.S.S. *Renville* in Batavia Harbor and took its name from that fact, it appeared that peace finally would be allowed to break out again. A United Nations Committee was kept on the spot. United Nations military observers were assigned to report on the observance, or nonobservance, of the military truce.

But again the Dutch decided to take matters into their own hands. On December 18, 1948, while the rest of the Western World was getting ready to celebrate Christmas, and while the Republic was still busy suppressing a Communist rebellion, the Dutch tore up the Renville agreement, which had not been implemented anyway, and sent their troops in to finish the job they had started eighteen months before. This time they went on to the Republican capital of Jogjakarta, arrested all the government leaders they could find, including the Republican president, Soekarno, and the vice president and premier, Mohammed Hatta, and seized control of all the territory they had troops to garrison.

This time there was no hesitation. The whole world was against the Dutch—Christian, Islamic, Communist. Finally they were forced to free the leaders and restore them to their capital. A new agreement was made, called the Van Royen–Roem Agreement, from the names of the two chief negotiators, and a round-table conference of representatives of all Indonesians and the Dutch was called for The Hague. There, after much bitterness, several deadlocks, and a succession of crises, the shape of the United States of Indonesia was finally agreed upon and the date for full sovereignty —January 1, 1950—was set.

The terms were less favorable to the Dutch than had been those either of the Linggadjati or the Renville agreements. And although outwardly they also appeared less favorable to the Republic, since the formation of several Dutch-sponsored new states was accepted in territory over which the Republic's *de facto* authority had been recognized in the two previous agreements, it remained by far the stronger of the several states of the new United States of Indonesia, and with the most powerful and best known leaders.

If the Dutch gained anything except monetary satisfaction from their military operations, it is impossible to determine what it was. What they did win was the almost unanimous censure of the civilized world. They won also the hatred of many Indonesians. They gave to the Communists in Indonesia and the rest of Asia a propaganda weapon the Red legions could never have forged themselves. They lost economic advantages that were theirs in both the Linggadjati and Renville agreements. They burdened their small and deficit country with a debt they will be years in paying off, if ever.

Why they acted as they did probably even a Dutchman could not satisfactorily explain. The ostensible reason was that the Republic was not living up to its side of the military bargain, and they felt they must go into Republican territory and restore law and order for the people toward whom they professed a responsibility.

That reason may have been a valid one for the first action, although there was evidence even then that violations of truce lines were being made by both Indonesians and Dutch military units. Why they launched the second one must remain a puzzle. They knew that the United Nations had before it reports from its military observers that although there were violations by the Republicans, there was a good suspicion that they were not unwelcome to some of the Dutch commanders and that many of them had been distorted by Dutch propagandists far beyond their real significance. They knew also that they had not even attempted to implement many of the provisions of the Renville Agreement and that this fact was clear on the record at United Nations Headquarters at Lake Success, New York.

The Dutch knew that they would be going against world opinion if they defied not only their own written agreement but the expressed wishes of the United Nations Security Council. They had before them, too, the example of French Indo-China, where the French had not been successful in three years in subjecting a much less cohesive, more poorly armed insurgent movement. When, in the face of this evidence, they pressed ahead with a new military campaign, they lost a prize that could have been theirs for the taking with a different approach, and they placed a black page in their history that cannot be erased.

A private evaluation of Dutch actions by a former high United Nations official just prior to the second "police action" had this to say, in part:

Delay in negotiations for the implementation of the agreement upon the most specious pretext has apparently become the deliberate policy of the Dutch Government. The civil liberties promised in the Renville Agreement have been continuously denied by the Dutch. The promised restoration of trade has been delayed and delayed. The promise to use the assistance of the Committee of Good Offices in fulfilling the Agreement has had little or no fulfillment. The Republic has no representation in a provisional government.

After ten months since the acceptance of the basic principles of freedom and self-determination, there have been no steps looking toward the promised plebiscite or other forms of free elections for the self-determination of the Indonesian peoples as to whether they wish to join the Republic or some other State in the promised all-inclusive federal United States of Indonesia. There have been no steps for the calling of a constitutional convention with representation to be based on population as provided in the Renville Agreement. The main thing wrong with the Renville Agreement is its nonfulfillment. The chief cause of this is Dutch intransigence.

Despite the defects of a revolutionary young Republic and despite the frustrations of the hopes of the people of the Republic, mainly due to the failures of the Dutch to join hands to fulfill the promises of the Renville Agreement, the Republic of Indonesia has crushed a Communist revolt and has survived to this hour against the terrific odds of the Dutch delays, the naval blockade, the unilateral political fragmentation, and the economic strangulation.

A modern sovereign nation such as the Kingdom of the Netherlands would be truer to its great democratic traditions of tolerance and freedom by seeking to find ways and means of facilitating the implementation of the basic principles promised in the Renville Agreement. Tragically for its own good name and for the cause of freedom in the world, the Government of the Netherlands seems to be intent on a deliberate policy of finding every pretext for delay in the fulfillment of an Agreement which cooperatively promised much for the future well-being of the people of Indonesia and the people of the Netherlands.

The people of the Netherlands could give a new lift to the hopes of freedom all over this still hopeful world by seeking ways to fulfill rather than pretexts to delay and betray the hopes of the Republic and the people of Indonesia. The present Government of the Netherlands would serve better the cause of freedom with good faith and good will in the prompt implementation of the Renville Agreement in accordance with the suggestion from the Committee of Good Offices. The present Netherlands Government, in rising above being a victim of its own propaganda against the Republic of Indonesia, should no longer delay fulfilling the democratic promises of the Renville Agreement, should stop making a mockery of the Agreement worked out through the good offices of the United Nations, and should quit serving the monstrous cause of both the imperialistic and the totalitarian foes of democracy in this critical hour for freedom in the modern world.

That is a hard judgment on the Dutch but one which has been verified by most neutral observers. "If we play our cards right," a member of the staff of one Dutch official quoted his chief as saying just before the first military action, "we can stay here for another hundred years." Whether apocryphal or true, it neatly expresses what was the Dutch record between 1946 and 1949.

There is no questioning that the East Indies was a large prize and worth a large risk, even a loss of the respect of the rest of the world. Indonesia had furnished the Dutch for over three hundred years, directly and indirectly, between 15 per cent and 25 per cent of their national income; that is, the difference between prosperity and a high standard of living—one of the highest in Europe—or a low standard and international impotence. The House of Orange was the richest royal house and Queen Wilhelmina one of the world's richest women. The islands furnished some 250,000 Dutchmen resident there a fine living they could hardly have won elsewhere with their own efforts. The strategic raw materials of the Indies—tin, rubber, oil, quinine, copra—gave the Dutch an international position to which they otherwise had no claim. It was while trying to find a new and shorter route to the riches of the Indies that Christopher Columbus discovered the Western Hemisphere.

The islands of Indonesia, or the Dutch East Indies as they were known for so many centuries, are an extension of the Asiatic mainland. They stretch for 2,500 miles from the Malay Peninsula to the sixth continent, Australia. The principal islands, or groups, that were under the Dutch flag are Sumatra, Java, Bali, Madoera, part of Borneo, part of New Guinea, the Moluccas, and the Celebes. Superimposed on a map of the United States with Sumatra on the state of Washington, Dutch New Guinea runs beyond Florida, the southeasternmost state.

Java is the most populous of the islands, with an estimated population in 1945 of 50,000,000, and the main rice-producing land. Its terraced rice fields are one of the engineering wonders of the world and are hundreds of years old. Sumatra is the oil island, where are the wells and refineries that make it the principal oil-producing area of the Far East. The tin mines, which were largely a government operation, are on Billiton, Bangka, and Riaw, all small islands off Java's north coast, and on Sumatra.

Militarily, Indonesia occupies a strategic position as a land bridge from Asia, from which it is separated only by the Strait of Malacca, to Australia. It stands as a barrier between the two, as it proved to be during the Japanese war. Ethnologically, it is primarily Malayan. Religiously, it is predominantly Moslem, to which sect belong an estimated 90 per cent of its 72,000,000 people, making the United States of Indonesia the largest Moslem state, its population being 30 per cent greater than that of the second largest, Pakistan. It is the southeasterly extremity of a Moslem world that stretches down from its origin in the Mediterranean basin through the Arab States, Afghanistan, Pakistan, and Malaya to the white, and Christian, continent of Australia. There are 2,500,000 Christians and 1,000,000 Buddhists.

Indonesia's history goes back thousands of years. At one time Java was the center of a kingdom that included most of Southeast Asia. Some fifty kilometers out of the Republican capital of Jogjakarta is an ancient, beautifully carved Buddhist shrine called Borabodur that was built, it is believed, in the eighth century, or seven hundred years before Columbus discovered the Americas. In Indonesia have been found some of the earliest relics of man from the mid-Pleistocene Age. Indonesia first became linked with Europe through the early Portuguese explorers, in the fifteenth and sixteenth centuries. (Portugal today retains only part of the small island of Timor, halfway between Java and New Guinea.) The Dutch sailors drove out the Portuguese in the seventeenth century; and except for a brief period during which the English disputed the Dutch claims, during the early nineteenth century, it was Dutch until the Indonesians decided to claim their ancient land for themselves and proved strong enough to do it.

The Dutch have always made the claim that they were the world's finest colonial administrators. That is like saying that a man is a good husband because he always beat his wife with a rubber hose instead of with a club and therefore left few scars on her. Colonialism always is exploitation, no matter how it may be coated with sugary words. (The United States has its own not too clean record in the Philippines, Samoa, Guam, and Puerto Rico, although all have been set free, or are being freed, without coercion from outside, or revolt from within.)

The best test of colonialism is whether the governing power has educated the colonial people and prepared them for self-rule. The Dutch record in Indonesia is, in that respect, no better than that of any other European country. In fact, it is not as good as that of the British. Literacy in Indonesia was only an estimated 7 per cent at the beginning of the Japanese war in 1941. There is today only one doctor for each 60,000 people. The Hague had promised eventual self-government to the Indonesians (although not until 1942, with the war well under way, was any definite, public commitment made by the Crown), but progress toward it was so slow as to be almost indistinguishable at times.

What is true among the Dutch claims is that they were far less brutal in their treatment of insurgents than were most colonial powers. But part of that record must be ascribed to the gentleness and sweetness of the Indonesians themselves. They made few insurrections against their Dutch masters. The Dutch also did not draw the color line matrimonially. Many of the Dutch civil servants, estate owners, and workers took Indonesian wives. Indonesian students in the Netherlands married and carried back to the islands Dutch wives.

But the Dutch never allowed any real nationalism to develop. Many of the present Republican leaders spent many years before the war in jail or in exile for political activities. The Republicans' first president, Soekarno, its first vice president, Mohammed Hatta, and its first premier, Soetan Sjahrir, all were in exile, and had been there for many years, when the Japanese attacked Pearl Harbor.

After the war the Dutch attempted to brand the Republican

leaders as Japanese collaborators and the Republic as a puppet creation of the Japanese militarists. That propaganda tack was abandoned when non-Dutch newspapermen began to go into the islands and to learn something of the history of the nationalist movement there and to study the records of the Republican leaders.

It is true that Soekarno and Hatta, of the four most prominent early Republican leaders, worked with the Japanese. That was a marriage of convenience, as they have since often declared and as the record shows. They, Sjahrir and the late Amir Sjariffoedin, the fourth member of the Big Four, all were anti-Japanese before the start of the war. They saw in the quick defeat of the Dutch, and the Japanese occupation, an opportunity to promote the nationalism to which they had devoted their lives and for which they suffered in prison and in exile at Dutch hands. Sjahrir and Sjariffoedin, in fact, were active leaders of anti-Japanese sentiment during the years from 1942 to 1945, the latter being arrested and sentenced to death by the Japanese for his activities. He was only saved from death through the intervention of Hatta, who, while pretending willing collaboration, kept in touch with the other nationalists who refused to have any dealings with the men of Nippon.

Two days after the capitulation of the Japanese, on August 17, 1945, in the front yard of the home Soekarno was occupying in Batavia, was proclaimed the Republic of Indonesia. The organization that Soekarno and Hatta had built openly as a collaborating agency, and the underground group which Sjahrir, Sjariffoedin, Dr. A. J. Gani, and others had built up secretly through the years immediately moved in to disarm the Japanese, to release from internment the several thousand Dutchmen who had surrendered with little fighting three and one-half years before, and to establish a government. The red and white flag of the Republic flew from windows and from flagpoles all over the islands.

When the British troops, to whom had been entrusted the job of disarming the Japanese and reestablishing order in the Indies, finally arrived in Batavia six weeks after the surrender, they found a functioning government. Much to the anger and to the disgust of the Dutch, they treated the Republic as a going concern. With the return from Australia of the fugitive Netherlands Indies Government, headed by Dr. Hubertus J. van Mook as acting governor general, and the arrival of more and more Dutch troops, open fighting broke out all over Java and in Sumatra.

There seems no question who was responsible for the fighting. It was the Republicans. They were not well organized. The Japanese arms they had gained, either by surrender of Japanese forces to them or through overpowering small Japanese garrisons, were scattered among many small groups who took orders only from their local commanders. But there was also the factor of independence. The Indonesians saw the Dutch building up their military forces every day, calling their leaders Japanese puppets, promising them autonomy only in some future time that was as vague as are most governmental promises of reform.

Attacks began against both the Dutch and the British garrisons in the port cities. The Republican leaders shifted their capital from Batavia to Jogjakarta, and by inference, if not directly, gave assent to the effort to drive the European troops into the sea. In Soerabaja several hundred Dutch civilians were murdered, or died later from ill treatment. Brigadier Mallaby, the British commander at Soerabaja, was shot and killed by a Republican, resulting in quick and terrible retaliation by the British. One small Indonesian city near Batavia was leveled by British fighter and bomber planes.

Streets of British or Dutch-occupied towns became unsafe at night for white men. Concilitory Indonesian leaders were kidnaped, murdered, and their houses looted and burned. The British and Dutch threw gasoline on the flames by rearming Japanese troops, under whom the Indonesians had suffered much cruelty and constant indignities for three and one-half years, to aid in containing the Republican guerrillas.

There were two men to whom this tragic turn of events seemed madness. They were Sjahrir and Dr. van Mook. The latter, as acting governor general, flew to The Hague in February, 1946, to secure from his government permission to resume negotiations and to try and reach a peaceful settlement. The British sent in their top trouble-shooting diplomat, Sir Archibald Clark Kerr, now Lord Inverchapel. Negotiations were resumed.

The situation quieted through the summer as Sjahrir and Dr. van Mook, both having to guard their rear constantly as well as their front, patiently negotiated to work out the details of a settlement. Lord Killearn, British high commissioner for Southeast Asia, took over the role of mediator that had been established by Sir Archibald.

Truce lines were established around the British-held ports of Java and Sumatra, and the disarming and repatriation of the 300,000 Japanese troops that were in the islands was speeded up. As the Dutch troops came in, the British turned over to them their equipment and the responsibility for maintaining perimeter lines and patroling. In October a military truce was agreed upon. On November 15 the Linggadjati Agreement was signed and on November 30 the British troops moved out, leaving the islands in Dutch and Indonesian hands.

Thus the situation remained through the winter, with a framework drawn for a peaceful transition, but with heavy pressures working against the moderates on both sides. On the Republican side one of these divisive forces was General Soedierman, the commander in chief. Others were the leaders of the independent military forces—then numbering about 250,000 men on the island of Java—who paid little attention to orders from Jogjakarta. And, of course, there were always the Communists, led by Alemin, and the Trotskyites, led by Tan Malaka. The latter had been jailed in the spring after an unsuccessful attempt to force Sjahrir, who was kidnaped and held prisoner for several days, into declaring all-out war on the Dutch. Soekarno and Hatta forced Sjahrir's release and jailed the conspirators.

On the Dutch side were the military leaders in Indonesia, led by the late General Spoor and by Admiral Pinke, both of whom wanted to move in and "put these rebellious natives in their place"; and back home were the old colonials and imperialists, led by Dr.

Romme, the Catholic party leader, who called van Mook a traitor for dealing with the Republicans.

Although the Linggadjati Agreement finally was accepted by both governments and was initialed on March 25, 1947, in Rijswijk Palace in Batavia, relations rapidly deteriorated. On July 20, van Mook pushed the button on the "police action," motivated by only he knows what political ambitions and sum of irritations, and the Indonesian question became an international, instead of a Dutch, problem.

The cause of the Indonesian case is simple: the desire of a people for their independence. For over three hundred years they had seen the riches of their country being used for the purposes of a European nation, not for the betterment of their own condition. They were in no mood for delay, especially after having established to their own satisfaction that they did have the leadership, and the ability, to govern.

The Dutch desire for slower transition is more complex. Five years of occupation of their homeland by the Germans, and the destruction done during liberation, had left them with great problems of reconstruction which they could hardly carry out without the revenue from the Indies that had sustained them for so long. Every day of delay in working out the agreement meant that much more actual loss of revenue. And not only denial of a return, but also actual expenditure in maintaining over 100,000 troops in Indonesia and supporting the economy of the port cities that were held. This latter figure was between $1,500,000 and $3,000,000 a day. Instead of being a source of revenue, Indonesia was a liability.

Entering also into the picture, say many who have studied Dutch history and the Dutch character, is the Calvinistic fervor with which the Dutch attack a problem once they have decided on a course they can justify to their conscience. They believed they were offering the Indonesians a fair settlement and they would not budge beyond a certain point. The outraged protests from other peoples when they attempted to impose their own solution by force shocked them.

Among the Dutch leaders in the Indies, there was the additional psychological factor of war nerves. Many of the military figures had spent years of internment by the Japanese. After being humiliated for years, they were in a mood to do some knocking around themselves. Many had lost friends or relatives in the Soerabaja "massacre," as they called it, or in the fighting around Batavia, Bandoeng, and other places. The families of some of the Dutch officers were not released by the Republicans until eighteen months after the end of the war.

There was an additional and little publicized element in the situation, where events have proven the Dutch to be right. That was a desire on the part of many people in the Indies, notably among the Sundanese of West Java, for a more decentralized state than was promised them by the Republic. They recognized the great service that had been done by the Republican leaders but they did not relish domination from Batavia by a Republican government any more than they had liked domination by a Dutch colonial government based there.

The almost twoscore states that finally evolved to make up the United States of Indonesia probably came much closer to meeting the desires of the people and eliminating friction in the future than would have the three envisaged in the Linggadjati Agreement, of which the Republic would have been overwhelmingly dominant, not only politically, but economically as well.

The United States of Indonesia has some difficult times ahead. It took over a large debt from the Netherlands Indies Government. The scorched-earth policy adopted by the Republicans during the two "police actions" destroyed many stocks of raw materials that were piled up during the war and since, and left many factories and estates in a sorry condition.

But the Indies have so many things that the world needs that there is no question of finding markets once its economy is again operating freely and with no threat of war.

Led by such men as Soekarno, Sjahrir, Hatta, Dr. Roem, Dr. Soemitro, the able young economist who was sent to the United

States in 1947 to interest United States capital in Indonesia, and hundreds of others, no less inclined toward the West and democratic in their political outlook, the Republic should give the world no cause for fear that Indonesia will line up with the Communists. If there had been any real movement in that direction, it would have materialized more strongly than it did during the anxious years while the United States of Indonesia was having its painful birth. The estimated 1,000,000 Chinese do not have the importance in Indonesia that they have elsewhere in Southeast Asia, because they are an insignificant minority among Indonesia's increasing millions.

In today's world Indonesia hardly can be expected to develop as rapidly as did the United States during the late eighteenth and early nineteenth centuries. But the analogy between the birth of the two countries is close. Their development could be no less parallel. A new and vital force took its place in Asia on December 28, 1949.

PART VI. THE EAST INDIES

CHAPTER 2. *Indonesia's Founding Fathers*

It is difficult to think of the small, smiling men with the soft voices and soft hands, who have made a nation of a colony of uneducated people, as the fathers of anyone or of anything. But the analogy between what they have done in Indonesia and what the men the United States calls its "Founding Fathers" did in the former British colonies in North America is a valid one.

The outward softness and the conciliatory attitude of the men who won Merdeka (freedom) for the people of the East Indies is a misleading indication of their real fiber. They are as tough-minded as Jefferson, Hamilton, Franklin, Washington, and the others who founded the United States of America. They are no less determined to make real their dream of a United States of Indonesia. Through years of Dutch persecution, which saw many of them imprisoned or exiled, and four years of brutal Japanese occupation, they did not waver from their announced program. Through more years of vacillation by the Western democracies and attempts by the Dutch to impose their own solution of Indonesia's future, they never wavered from their demand for independence, for the right of the people of Indonesia to benefit from the riches of their own country and to decide their own destiny.

It is a little early properly to assess the historical places of men like Soekarno, Sjahrir, Hatta, Sjariffoedin, Hadji Agoes Salim, Roem, Anak Agung, the Sultan of Djokja and others. Oftentimes it is found that a comparatively obscure man, through his influence on better known public leaders, has exercised a considerably greater influence than he is credited with in his time. Still, it is possible to make some valid assessments now of roles played.

The four who cannot be left off any list and whose influence on the course of Indonesian nationalism is unquestioned are Soekarno, Sjahrir, Hatta, and Sjariffoedin. All were active in the prewar years in promoting Indonesian nationalism. All spent many years in jail or in exile for their beliefs before the Japanese came to drive out the Dutch temporarily and give them the opportunity to build the organization that became, on August 17, 1945, the declared Republic of Indonesia and is now the dominant part of the sovereign United States of Indonesia.

They complement each other in many ways. Soekarno is the political leader, the orator, the public figure, and probably not a very profound thinker. Sjahrir is the intellectual, in whom East and West meet, the one who was always willing to sacrifice a momentary advantage if he thought it would lead to a long-term gain. Hatta and Sjariffoedin, before the latter became discouraged with the West and turned to Marxism—no long step for a socialist—were the administrators, the practical men who made realities of the dreams and philosophies of the other two.

All but Soekarno, who was born in Soerabaja, on Java's north coast, came from one or another of the tough hill tribes of Sumatra. Opposition to outside rule was born in them. The Dutch never attempted, except in the oil fields along the Sumatran coast, to place their ancestors under the same strict rule that was employed in Java, Bali, Madoera, the Celebes, and the Moluccas, the more thickly populated islands of the Indies.

When they proclaimed the Republic in 1945, all were relatively young men. Soekarno, the eldest, was only forty-four years of age, Hatta was forty-three, Sjariffoedin was thirty-eight, and Sjarhrir was thirty-six. (Washington was forty-three when the Declaration of Independence was signed in 1775, Jefferson was thirty-two, and John Adams was thirty-six. Franklin was the only patriarch among the leaders; he was sixty-nine. But he had young ideas.)

Soekarno is tall, as Indonesians stand—about five feet six or seven inches. He is a handsome man by any standards, with a warming smile. He has a firm handclasp. Oratorical phrases come to him as easily as they did to Roosevelt, or do to Churchill. He is inspired by a crowd, as are all great orators, and he enjoys his mastery of people in mass. He can play on the emotions of a crowd of Indonesians as Heifetz does on the strings of a violin, carrying them with him from tears to laughter or anger, and back again.

One of the chief bases of the charge of collaboration with the Japanese that the Dutch used against him and the other Republican leaders was the record of the speeches that he made during the Japanese occupation. His own explanation of the fervor of some of his addresses was that it was necessary to arouse in his fellow Indonesians the spirit of nationalism that they had lacked under the relatively benevolent rule of the Dutch. Those who know him well ascribe the intensity of his language to a disease not uncommon among orators—rapture with the sound of their own voices. He is always quick to sense the mood of his audience and to play on it. If the mood was one of admiration for the Japanese for the ease with which they had driven the white colonials out of Southeast Asia, then Soekarno was not the man to overlook that theme.

The Indonesians' first president was born of a well-to-do family, who could afford to educate him, on June 6, 1901. He went through the primary and secondary schools of Java and took a degree in engineering (from which comes the Dutch title Ir., that so often has been wrongly given in American publications as Dr.) from the Technical School of Bandoeng. He set up an engineering office at Bandoeng, but he did not practice his profession for long.

Like most young educated Indonesians, he was a swift convert to nationalism. When, in 1927, he helped form and became the outstanding leader of the Indonesian nationalist organization, the Partai Nasional Indonesia, he was arrested by the Dutch and exiled. He was allowed to return to Java in 1932, apparently in the belief he had reformed; but a year of pamphlet writing and work in the Partindo, or Party of Greater Indonesia, convinced the Dutch he was a dangerous man to have around and they banished him again to Sumatra, to what probably would have been permanent exile had it not been for the war. The Japanese freed Soekarno when they took Sumatra and, recognizing his position and his abilities, set him up as head of the various collaborating bodies of Indonesians they formed and disbanded and reformed during the three and one-half years of their occupation of the Indies.

Soekarno has impressed those Westerners who have met him (some of whom believe they know him well), as a brilliant but erratic man, without Hatta's toughness or administrative ability and lacking the ability for clear and philosophical thinking that Sjahrir has. But he is a great Indonesian leader in his own way. It is certain none of the others have had, or probably could win, the general public approval and pride that is his.

Sjahrir is an unassuming little man, only five feet tall, of whom real appreciation comes only with long acquaintance. He laughs easily and often, and he is inclined to understatement. There can be no doubt, however, that he was the real thinker of the revolution.

No one can read his book *Out of Exile*, which was published in the United States in 1948 and, in part, in the Netherlands in 1945 and not realize that here is a first-class mind in operation. The larger part of it is composed of letters he wrote to his Dutch wife—to whom he has since given a divorce so that she might marry his brother—while he was in exile, first in the steaming, malarial, Dutch internment camp of Boven Digoel, on New Guinea, and then on the more pleasant island of Banta.

Sjahrir was only twenty-four when he was arrested by the Dutch in 1934 for having been active in an organization promoting education among the Indonesians. He was held in jail for five months without any charges being placed against him. ("As a native," he said in one of his letters to Mrs. Sjahrir, "I have no rights to assert.") Then a hearing lasting one hour was held, during which he was allowed no counsel and no defense, and he was sentenced to indeterminate exile at Boven Digoel. Exiled with him was Hatta.

For over a year the two young Indonesians, both educated in

Holland, idealistic, earnest, decent, lived in conditions that were as close to Dante's Inferno as it is possible to imagine. They were on a near-starvation diet, which could be increased only by foreswearing their political convictions, living in huts they made themselves in a malarial rain forest. Both contracted the disease while imprisoned there. They were fortunate. Many of the internees went insane.

In February, 1936, they were shifted to Banda Neira, in the Molucca Islands, after they had signed statements agreeing they would not engage in any political activity there. Much was made in Java by the Dutch of these statements, which were interpreted to mean that they had forsaken the cause of Indonesian nationalism, which neither had. That was proven by the fact that the Dutch continued to keep them in exile for six years more.

When the Japanese attacked in December, 1941, the Dutch suddenly awoke to the realization that if they were to rally the Indonesians to their side, they had better bring back from exile some of their leaders. Accordingly, in January, 1942, Hatta and Sjahrir, the latter with three children from among many he had been teaching during his exile on Banda and whom he wished to adopt, were flown back to Java in a United States Navy Catalina flying boat that had left Ambon just ahead of the Japanese.

Neither Sjahrir nor Hatta had any illusions as to what "liberation" by the Japanese would mean. Both had decided that the militarists in Tokyo were cut from the same cloth as the Nazis and the Fascists. Hatta had written his views, which were widely circulated in Java by the Dutch. Oddly, the Japanese either did not appreciate the significance of the pamphlet or else they believed in Hatta's apparent conversion, for they accepted him as Soekarno's right-hand man.

Sjahrir, Hatta, and Soekarno, in conversations among themselves before the Japanese arrived, decided that the former should remain out of any collaborationist organizations and should work independently to organize Indonesians for the day of independence they hoped was coming now that the Dutch had been driven out.

Although under constant suspicion and occasional surveillance, Sjahrir was not arrested by the Japanese. During the last days just before capitulation he was sought by them; but by keeping on the move, and protected by the members of the organization he had built during the previous three years, he managed to remain free.

It was he who urged Soekarno and Hatta to declare the Republic on August 17, 1945, and he became chairman of the Working Committee of the appointed National Committee that was set up to serve as a representative legislative and governing body until a Congress could be elected. Later, when it was decided that a European type of government, instead of one patterned on that of the United States, was more suitable for Indonesia, he became the first premier of the Republic.

Sjahrir was born in the Minangkabau region of Sumatra's west coast on March 5, 1909. Like his three colleagues, his family had sufficient funds to send him to the primary and secondary schools in the islands and then to the Netherlands to study law at the University of Leyden. He was deeply impressed, while living in the Netherlands, with Western culture. He married there a Dutch girl, from whom he was separated for fourteen years during internment and war. When they finally met again in India, in 1945, he learned that she and the brother to whose care he had entrusted her were in love and he agreed to a divorce so that they might marry.

While still a student at Leyden and before he had secured his degree, Sjahrir decided that his place was back home in Indonesia and he returned there in 1932. He had been active in Indonesian student groups at Leyden and on his return to the Indies he joined the Pendidikan Nasional Indonesia, or Society for National Indonesian Education. It was for his activities in that organization that the Dutch arrested and then exiled him.

Sjahrir is a philosopher, but not an ascetic. He loves to dance and to play tennis. His young colleagues remember that in the early days of the Republic, after they had all been laboring for twelve to sixteen hours over paper work in their offices, Sjahrir would order them all to drop their work and go somewhere with him to dance and sing and laugh. He knows that man does not live on work alone.

Sjahrir resigned the premiership in June, 1947, when the cabinet split on his proposed settlement with the Dutch, and remained somewhat in the background for several years with the title only of adviser to the president. He remained the philosopher of the revolution, however, and a tremendous influence on the thinking, especially of the young intellectuals on whom the future of Indonesia depends. He heads his own party, which can be described as right-wing socialist.

Hatta has been from the very beginning the strong man of the Republic, the one who has the complete confidence of Soekarno and on whom the latter greatly depends. He is not much larger than Sjahrir, but where the latter gives an impression of softness, almost flabbiness, Hatta is built like a rock.

His career paralleled that of Sjahrir until the Japanese occupation. Both are Sumatrans. They both studied in the Netherlands. They were arrested at about the same time and spent eight years together in exile, at Boven Digoel and on Banda.

But whereas Sjahrir always was the philosopher, even when he was in his teens and early twenties, Hatta was always the man of action. He attached himself to Soekarno at the beginning of the Japanese occupation and was called to Saigon with Soekarno to see Count Terauchi just before the surrender. It was he who, at Sjahrir's urging, practically forced Soekarno to proclaim the Republic just two days after the capitulation, when the latter still was fearful of the strength of the Japanese. The story was told, but not confirmed by the principals, that Hatta had physically to restrain Soekarno from leaving Batavia when the British came. In view of Soekarno's long record of national leadership, and his willingness to suffer exile rather than to surrender his principals, the authenticity of that story seems doubtful. But it indicates the thinking of the Indonesians about their first vice president.

Mohammed Hatta was born at Bukit Tinggi, Sumatra, in 1902.

While still in his teens he organized a nationalist Sumatran Youth Organization. His extracurricular activities while a student in the Netherlands, from 1925 to 1931, seems to have been fully as intensive as were his studies. He was a leader of the Liga party, an international student movement against colonialism and imperialism, for several years, and attended the International Democratic Congress in Paris in 1926 as the representative for Indonesia, and the Liga Congress in Brussels in 1927.

On his return to Indonesia in 1927 he continued his nationalist activities there, working with Sjahrir in the educational movement and editing the newspaper *Indonesia Merdeka.* His arrest and banishment came in 1934.

Since his appointment as vice president in 1945 and his election as premier in 1947, he has held aloof from party politics, but he is, like Sjahrir, a socialist, and like Soekarno, a Moslem.

The tragic figure of the quartet who created the Republic is Amir Sjariffoedin, the only Christian of the four. In his person was something of the attitudes and the attributes of both Sjahrir and Hatta. He was an idealist and a thinker like Sjahrir. But also he was an able, hard-headed administrator like Hatta. This was shown in his administration of the Department of Defense. He took a ragtag, poorly armed, poorly organized group of boys and young men who had become little more than bandits and was rapidly welding them into a well disciplined army when the Dutch began their first military action on July 20, 1947. The Dutch action forced him to let the army break up into guerrilla bands with little central direction or authority.

Sjariffoedin's defection to the Communists in the fall of 1948 and his announcement that he had been secretly a Communist for many years is a complete mystery to his many close associates and friends in the Republican government. They cannot rationalize the defection. They do not believe the admission. His execution, after the Communist revolt had been suppressed, was carried out by a local commander before Hatta's orders to spare him were received.

Neither Hatta nor any of Sjariffoedin's other friends believe that he was when he died a Communist, or that he ever had been. He was a sincere Christian, who served as a lay preacher nearly every Sunday despite the burdens of his office. The two "religions" do not mix. Their belief is that he became so disillusioned with the Western powers, and especially with the vacillating policy of the United States toward the Dutch military actions, that he reluctantly decided Moscow was the best hope, and declared himself a Communist to solicit that aid for realization of his dreams.

Sjariffoedin was born in Medan, Sumatra, in 1907. Like Sjahrir and Hatta he went to the Netherlands for his college work, studying at both the University of Leyden and at Haarlem. He took his law degree in 1933 at the Batavia Law School and the same year was arrested and sentenced to two years in prison for his nationalist writings.

After his release from prison in 1935 he practiced law in West Java until the fall of the Netherlands in 1940, when he accepted the offer of a government post, as an adviser to the Department of Economic Affairs. He was later Secretary of the Export Bureau and then editor of the *Economic Weekly*, published by the Department of Economic Affairs.

Sjariffoedin accepted these tasks with the colonial government, he told his friends, because he was more opposed to national socialism, as exemplified in Germany and Italy and Japan, than he was with the type of colonialism practiced by the Dutch. It did not mean that he had given up hope of eventual independence for Indonesia. But he believed that eventually could be attained by peaceful means. In the meantime, he thought the democracies should be sustained.

Sjariffoedin remained an implacable foe of the Japanese after the occupation, working in the underground against them. He finally was arrested and sentenced to death, a sentence that Hatta was able to have commuted to life imprisonment. Which, incidentally, was one reason why Hatta says he agreed to collaborate, so that he might be in a position to render aid to those of his secret colleagues who might be arrested by the Japanese.

Sjariffoedin was released after the Japanese capitulation and the declaration of the Republic, and was appointed minister of information. When Sjarhir became premier in November, 1945, Sjariffoedin remained in that job for a time, but when the cabinet was reorganized, he was elevated to minister of defense, one of the key posts and one of the most difficult ones because most of the irregulars fighting for the Republic operated much as they pleased.

Working sixteen hours a day, Sjariffodein set out to whip these guerrilla bands of wild boys into a disciplined military force. He knew that the Dutch would recognize force more quickly than they would reason. By January, 1947, Sjariffoedin had enrolled almost 100,000 in the regular Republican Army and had secured from the others a census of arms, which was not in itself important, but was the first obeisance to central authority they had made. Then the Dutch police action scattered them, and Sjariffoedin lost heart.

He had built better than he knew, however. When he threw in his destiny, along with Setaidjit, with the Moscow exile Mucha and the Communists, the regular army remained loyal to the Republic. They suppressed the revolt and finally caught and executed Sjariffoedin himself.

Sjariffoedin was married and the father of two children. He lived simply and frugally in a small house in Jogjakarta, the Republican capital. His turning to the Communists was a cruel blow to the Republic, since it gave its enemies good ammunition for the international propaganda battle. It was a harder blow to his friends, who still mourn his death and the nature of it.

The man who can be said to have succeeded Sjariffoedin as the fourth member of the Big Four was Dr. Mohammed Roem, an Indonesian-educated lawyer, who was minister of interior in both Sjahrir's and Sjariffoedin's cabinets. He attained international prominence when he negotiated with van Royen the agreement that led to the convocation of the round-table conference at The Hague in the fall of 1949 where the final blueprint for Indonesian sovereignty was drawn.

Dr. Roem is no bigger than Sjahrir, a would-be physician who changed in midcourse to the law. He is, however, as the Dutch can substantiate, an able negotiator and a brilliant student of government. A Moslem, he has been for several years one of the leaders of Indonesia's largest political party, the Masjoemi.

No calling of the roll of Indonesian leaders—no matter what unfairness may be done to many younger men who worked tirelessly, but mostly behind the scenes—is complete without the name of Hadji Agoes Salim, the wise and witty little Moslem leader, who, at the age of sixty-one in 1945, can be called the Benjamin Franklin of the Indonesian Revolution. He succeeded Sjahrir as foreign minister in 1947, when the latter relinquished that post along with the premiership. Because of his many friendships among the leaders of the Arab States and the Moslems of India, he was able to rally international support to the cause of the Republic.

Long before he had the foreign ministry post, however, old Hadji was a tempering force within the inner circle. When tempers became strained, he always could be depended on, intimates said, to make some witty saying that would dissolve the argument in laughter. When it was resumed, it was done in better temper.

A Sumatran, old Hadji—as that title indicates—has made the pilgrimage to Mecca. He made it while a young man, by sailing ship, camel back, and on foot. He remarked after a trip to Mecca in 1946 that he had flown in one hour on one leg of the journey over territory it had taken him twenty-eight days to cross on his early journey forty years before.

Hadji had only a meager formal education, but he had read widely and assimilated much wisdom through the years in his career as government interpreter and translator—he speaks several languages impeccably, including English—and as newspaper writer and editor. Although a Moslem, he, like many other leaders of that sect, does not practice all he preaches, enjoying both tobacco and liquors when they are available. Widely read, widely traveled, he is the most cosmopolitan of the top Republican command.

There are many others, such as Dr. A. K. Gani, the "glamour boy" of the revolution, who has been both a hospital administrator and movie actor and who served as economics minister and later as vice premier, who have played important parts in the early days, but more in the role of assistants than of real leaders either of thought or of action.

Because of their small size, which is characteristic of most of the people of Southeast Asia, and their outward appearance of softness, many Westerners probably are inclined to underestimate on first meeting the men who made Merdeka. Three hundred and fifty years of a rule that was little opposed had made the Dutch contemptuous of them. The Dutch learned, to their sorrow, what kind of men they were. The rest of the West would do well not to underestimate them if they decide to extend their influence into Malaya, into Sarawak, Brunei, and British Borneo. Many of them hold the dream, clear in their minds, of a free, sovereign, and united Southeast Asia that includes all those lands.

PART VII. REPUBLIC OF THE PHILIPPINES

CHAPTER 1. *Experiment in Colonialism*

When Commodore George Dewey led his little squadron of gunboats and cruisers into Manila Bay on the morning of May 1, 1898, and there defeated the Spanish squadron of Admiral Montojo in the decisive Far Eastern battle of the Spanish-American War, he helped to launch the United States as a colonial power. Forty-eight years, two months, and four days later—on July 4, 1946—the United States liquidated that venture by granting the Philippines full independence. For the first time in history a great white nation voluntarily had given a much smaller, much weaker nation its freedom.

The ties were not completely broken. How could they be? The Philippine Republic had just emerged from a war in which it had suffered more cruelly than any other invaded area of the Far East. Nearly all of its government buildings were in ruins. Its first free Congress had to meet in a former schoolhouse. For forty-eight years its economy had been tied to that of the United States. The United States could not immediately raise tariff barriers against its sugar and spices and tobacco and embroideries. There had to be a transition period. That was provided for in amendments to the Philippine Independence Act of 1934. These set the old prewar quotas on the Filipinos' principal exports to the United States, gave them free entry until 1954, and from then until 1972 a gradually increasing tariff.

There were conditions favorable to the United States in this act. The principal one was the granting of the right to American citizens to enter the Republic to "exploit"—an unfortunate choice of a word—the natural resources. It was attacked vigorously by some Filipino leaders, but the people themselves, in a referendum on that subject alone, voted overwhelming to grant that right. The Filipinos also granted to the United States the right to maintain military bases in their islands for the protection of the security of both countries. This also was attacked by the extreme nationalists and the Filipino Communists, but it was a good bargain for each. The United States maintains there today, as a matter of fact, only token naval, air, and ground forces. If another crisis should arise, however, the bases are there and the legal way is paved for their quick expansion and use.

These were all undertakings entered into freely by the government of the republic, and backed by a large majority of its people. Carlos P. Romulo, in his farewell speech in the United States Congress where he sat as the last resident commissioner of the Philippines during the year preceding the declaration of the republic, stated eloquently the attitude of the majority of the Filipinos when he said:

> You came to the Philippines by accident. . . . On July 4 the association comes to an end—but in its end is its beginning. For this is the final chapter of Book I, and on July 5 we begin the first chapter of Book II. This is the moment toward which we all have worked for so long and it is come at last. But brotherhood does not die when the younger brother reaches his maturity. It changes, it broadens, it deepens. That is what will happen between us.

Commissioner Romulo went on to spell out in more stirring detail than an American would have, what the past association had meant. By its statement of intentions when it assumed governance of the Philippines, he said, the United States "marked the beginning of the twentieth century with an experiment in brotherhood that is still going on." He continued:

> The idea was simple, as are all great truths. It was no more than this: that it is possible for a great and powerful nation to go into

a weak and poor land, to help educate its people, to teach the ways of modern democracy, to nurture and encourage and assist, and in the end to set a date for independence. And then to keep that date.

I put the idea into words and it sounds, perhaps, more trite than inspiring. That is because you, being an American, can afford to take it for granted. Ask the Filipino farmer why he took to the hills and harried the Japanese foe for three long years, and he will tell you of this idea, in his own simple way, and it will not sound trite. Ask the restless Indonesian what he thinks of the experiment in the Philippines and his answer will not be uninspired. Ask the man of Burma, or of Indo-China, or the native of India, or visit the troubled lands of the Middle East, and you will learn more about the Philippines than most Americans will ever know.

Mr. Romulo's speech presented, of course, the shinier, smoother side of the coin. There are cynics who will point out, and justifiably, that it took the United States long enough to get around to granting independence to the Filipinos. (Aguinaldo always believed that at his conference with Commodore Dewey in Hong Kong before the latter set out for the Battle of Manila that he was promised full and immediate independence for his people if he would continue the land attack against the Spanish in Manila that was already under way before the beginning of the Spanish-American War of 1898.) The amendments to the Philippine Independence Act still left Americans and American business in a preferred position in the Philippines. It will be many years before the Filipinos gain their full economic independence.

But contrast the American record in the Philippines, with all its shortcomings, against that of any other Western power in the Far East, or in any other colonial area, and the American record shines like a bright light in a dark world. In the first three postwar years the United States by direct and indirect means poured approximately $750,000,000 into the Philippines. The Army rebuilt roads and bridges and railroads destroyed during the war. It paid war-damage claims for buildings destroyed, and cared for wounded

Filipinos in its hospitals. Large loans were made by American agencies to help the Filipinos restore their country and to help it get started toward stability and full independence, economic as well as political.

All these things were not done selfishly. True, the beet-sugar growers of the United States were loud for Philippine independence. But it is a denial of the American spirit—and the charge comes largely from those with unclean hands, the colonial powers of Asia—to say that was the sole, or even the principal, reason why the Filipinos today walk proudly as free men in a free country, facing the future unafraid and able to speak their minds freely in the forums of the world.

There was a different atmosphere in Manila in February, 1947, than there was in the other cities of Asia. The president of the Republic of the Philippines sat in Malacanan Palace by right, and not by sufferance. The peso was stable at two for the American dollar, and there was no black market in Philippine currency. South of the Pasig River all was destruction, in what had been the loveliest part of the most beautiful city in the Orient (a commentary in itself on the beneficence of United States rule). But men were at work cleaning it up. It was not just lying there. There was a bustle and a vibrancy about the city that had been absent in Peiping, Shanghai, Nanking, Hong Kong, Singapore, Bangkok, and Batavia. There were no barricades on the outskirts of Manila. There was no sound of firing by night. No hostile glances followed a white man as he walked down the street. This was the Filipinos' land, and they knew it.

That the Philippines have a long and difficult road ahead cannot be denied. The country sustained actual war damage of between $750,000,000 and $1,000,000,000. They have little chance of getting much of that back as indemnity from Japan. As of January 1, 1949, the total of reparations received from Japan by the Philippines was $11,000,000. The sugar land and the sugar centrals were ruined. In 1946 imports were three times exports—$300,000,000 against $100,000,000.

It is estimated that 10 to 15 per cent of all the buildings in the Philippines were destroyed, either in the Japanese conquest of the Islands in 1941 and 1942 or in the recapture of them by the United States in 1944 and 1945. Another 10 to 15 per cent were damaged. There was hardly a major building left standing in Manila, a city of 675,000. Among the buildings destroyed or damaged were those most vital to the Philippine economy—the sugar mills, the warehouses, the copra drying sheds, the docks, and the schools. They were the solid structures that the Japanese used as war storage dumps or blockhouses and which had to be destroyed in the eviction of the Japanese from them.

Any evaluation of the Philippines, or of the Filipinos, must be made against this background of over three years of occupation and of more actual war damage than was suffered by any other area of the Far East except Japan itself.

Greater, perhaps, than the actual physical losses in the Philippines were the human ones and the moral breakdown that was almost inevitable with three and one-half years of war. Then there is the cancer of suspicion and of hatreds that was engendered between those who went into the hills to fight and live on half rations and those who stayed in the cities and collaborated in various degrees with the Japanese. After the war men who should have been working together to rebuild their shattered countries spent too much time hurling charges at each other.

The late Manuel Roxas, the last president of the commonwealth, the first president of the republic, was the principal target of the charge of collaboration, aside from those who were actually jailed, like Jorge Vargas and José Laurel. Every competent authority has said the charge against Roxas was an unjust charge. Manuel Quezon, first president of the commonwealth, who died of tuberculosis in the United States before his country was freed, told in his book *The Good Fight* that he had ordered Roxas to remain behind when he and General MacArthur left for Australia. Roxas was to mitigate as best he could the rigors of the occupation and was to lead the underground. General MacArthur gave him complete clearance. Nevertheless, until the very day of his death in the summer of 1948 while on an official inspection tour, the charge of collaborator followed him.

The death of Roxas was a great blow to the Philippines. Like most Spanish-speaking countries, the Philippines seemed to have a predeliction for following a *caudillo*, or a leader, rather than voting on issues in politics. Roxas fulfilled the role. He long had been recognized as Quezon's choice for his successor. He was a brilliant student of government, a fiery speaker, an able administrator.

On the shaded porch of beautiful Malacanan Palace, looking out over the Pasig River one bright morning in February, 1947, he talked, over the breakfast coffee cups, of his country and its problems.

The two major long-range problems—after necessary reconstruction—he said, were land-tenantry reform and industrialization. One of his first acts as president was to push through the Philippines Congress a new land rental law. In prewar times the rental largely had been one in three—one share for the tenant, one for the carabao (which the landlord generally owned), and one for the landlord. The law legalized the division as not more than 30 per cent for the landlord and the remainder to the tenant.

There was, too, the question of Church lands, although this was considerably exaggerated. Under Spanish rule the Catholic Church had been given enormous tracts of land, in both countryside and city. The Church did not administer these lands, or city holdings, directly but farmed them out to administrators at a fixed fee. The administrator's profit depended on how much he could charge above the guarantee. It was Roxas' plan, as soon as the money could be squeezed out of the budget, to buy up these lands and the city property—which included Manila's worst slum area—and sell at low interest rates to the tenants. The landlord rental law resulted in sale of much farm land. The government loaned the tenant, at low interest rates, the money to buy.

The second major problem was that of industrialization, to prepare the Philippines for the day when United States tariff bars would be up against Philippine sugar, the islands' major export crop in prewar days. This depended on power. There was little coal. The only other source was from the streams through large hydroelectric installations. This was costly, but elaborate plans were made for its full development. A start was largely dependent on the ability to buy needed equipment in the States.

This lack of available equipment, the hesitancy of foreign capital to invest in new enterprises in the Philippines, and the traditional disinclination of the Filipino with a little money to invest it in business for a reasonable return (he much prefers to lend it to his neighbor at an interest rate of 200 per cent or 300 per cent a year) all worked against President Roxas' program. The high prices for copra, hemp, and sugar on world markets also was a temptation to Philippines leadership to go back to the old agricultural economy. Vice President Quirino, who succeeded to the presidency on the death of Roxas, was not apparently as interested in the program of industrialization as had been his predecessor. Three years after the end of the war and a year after Roxas' death, the industrialization program had made little progress.

There was considerable doubt among some Filipinos that industrialization was the wiser course. Tomás Confessor, one of the Nationalist senators who had spent the war years as a guerrilla leader and was bitter in his denunciation of Roxas as a collaborator (which colored all his judgments), told me he believed the Republic of the Philippines would be better off as an agrarian state, catching fish and growing rice for its food staples and growing sugar, copra, and hemp and mining gold, chrome, and other metals for export.

At the end of the third peacetime year the trend was back to the old agricultural economy; industrialization had slowed almost to a halt. The factory equipment the Philippines had expected to receive from Japan as reparations had failed to materialize, and the prospects were poor that any equipment at all would be received from that source. American capital, probably because of the unrest elsewhere in Asia, was slow to migrate that close to the oncoming

Communist tide on the Asiatic mainland, and it was doubtful of a stable market there. Continuing high prices for sugar, copra, hemp, and other agricultural products made investment in agriculture more attractive.

This, of necessity, forced the government itself into the development of industry. In the immediate prewar era it controlled twenty different business and industrial corporations. It ran the Manila Hotel, owned and operated a brewery, operated public utilities, warehouses, docks, and transportation lines. President Quirino said that the government was anxious to dispose of many of these enterprises but could not find buyers. It did not, naturally, want to dispose only of its prosperous enterprises, for which buyers probably could have been found (seven of its twenty activities returning good profits).

Summarizing the economic picture after three years, Ford Wilkins, managing editor of the *Manila Bulletin*, an American-owned and operated newspaper and correspondent in the Philippines for the New York *Times*, put it this way in a dispatch to the *Times:*

> An over-all view of Philippine economic rehabilitation since the war shows the nation to be growing back into its pre-independence pattern and habits of trade, finance and economics. The Republic, in its third year of independence, has made progress toward stability. Its trade balance is on the road to equalization and the Quirino Administration says it has a balanced budget. Yet it faces the problem of economic survival after 1951. . . .
>
> The Philippines remains primarily an agricultural country. Economic thinkers who in the early post-war days sought to shift over the economy toward rapid industrialization have changed their minds. The wealth of the country, the kind of wealth that will see the nation through a crisis when money stops coming from the United States, lies not in manufacturing but in raw materials.
>
> This has been proved in many ways. Copra and its by-products, chiefly coconut oil, have proved the mainstay of the national income. When world prices were high, the Philippines cashed in. The industry is fully rehabilitated to the point of pre-war output in terms of income.
>
> The Philippines is rich in hardwoods. For two years the Govern-

ment virtually prohibited export because lumber was so needed for reconstruction. Now the ban has been partly lifted and export is once more possible. The lumber industry is the only one, except for copra, that has recovered to pre-war production levels, accounting for 35,000,000 pesos ($17,500,000) in output in 1948.

Three others have reached an estimated two-thirds recovery—rice, sugar and hemp. . . .

Rice is the staple crop. The Philippines, with plenty of adaptable land (which does not even need fertilizer to maintain productivity) and ready labor, never in history had produced enough rice for the needs of its own people. Rice production always has been in control of planters and middlemen, the latter largely Chinese, whose interests lay in keeping prices up and production scanty enough to achieve high prices.

President Quirino, recognizing the political dynamite in this situation, has sought to remedy it by establishing Government production control, but he has succeeded only in part.

The sugar industry is on the way to recovery as the country's richest source of revenue, but in a few years it will face an increasing duty in the United States market under the Philippine Trade Act of 1946 and will no longer be produced profitably (for export). Planters and millers are seeking government assistance. . . .

Filipinos in responsible governmental and business positions know that their country faces potentially thin times when United States funds from war damage and veterans' payments stop flowing freely in 1951. That is why they have been actively encouraging a flow of development capital from abroad without, however, any great success to date. Investment capital has responded to the rehabilitation of pre-war industries and ventures, but new and untried fields remain for the Government to tap.

Politically, the Philippines are more stable than any other part of Asia. The Communist-led agrarian revolt in Central Luzon that grew out of the wartime guerrilla organization—the Hukbalahaps—had degenerated in a year after the war largely to banditry. Some of the bands included United States Army deserters. They were a continual menace to peace in that area, camping out in the hills and raiding farms and villages and well armed with stolen United States arms, but they were not a political force. President Quirino treated with Luis Taruc, the Communist leader of the Huks in the summer of 1948, and promised amnesty for his followers if they would turn in their arms. Only a few score responded and Taruc disappeared back into the hills. Eventually, it appeared, the Philippine constabulary would run down the remnants of what once was a powerful movement, a movement which, however, received more attention in the United States than its importance in the Philippines warranted.

The collaboration issue also had become a dead letter. Collaboration never was clearly defined and the principal leaders never even were tried. Laurel, who had been outspokenly pro-Japanese even before the start of the war, and who headed the puppet government in Manila, was back making political speeches in 1949 and threatening a political comeback. His reacceptance, or at least tolerance, by the Filipinos affirmed anew their Spanish inclination to follow a persuasive leader rather than issues.

Although the emergence of some of the active wartime collaborators as accepted political figures might indicate an anti-American trend in the Philippines, few sober Americans familiar with Filipino habits of thought accepted it as such. What the attitude would be later, when the tariff walls began to go up, was something else. The United States then might become a target. The old ties, the remembrance of things past will not entirely disappear, however. Filipinos have only to look elsewhere in Asia to realize how well they themselves have been treated by a stronger Western power. The record has been written for history. A few political speeches, some economic strains, cannot erase it. And the United States Congress should be wise enough to keep that one placement of prestige and friendship in the Far East. If the Trade Act of 1946 appears to be endangering order in the Republic of the Philippines, it always can be amended.

The Philippines is one place in Asia where Americans can walk with pride and dignity. As General Romulo said, the Philippines is the United States' younger brother. When there is a crisis, brothers stick together.

PART VIII. THAILAND

CHAPTER 1. *Small Nation—Thailand (Siam)*

From a third-floor balcony of the impressive Ratokasindr Hotel in Bangkok, the gold-plated spires and domes of the palaces and shrines within the kingly compound that forms the heart of Thailand's capital city reflect on a clear night a thousand moons. Many of the rooftops are studded with jewels that so multiply the night light that a special radiance hangs over the seat of Thailand's king and government.

To an American or European visitor, Bangkok and the Siamese seem almost as exotic, as unreal, and as interesting today as they did to Anna Leonowens when she went to Thailand (or Siam as it was then called) a hundred years ago to teach the king's children and remained to influence his decisions and also to be taught herself some of the lessons the East still can impart to the West. As in Anna's days of verbal and mental jousting with the king, Thailand in this century still is a country 85 per cent agricultural, still with some of its dense forests unexplored, whose human landscape is dominated by yellow-robed, barefooted Buddhist priests with brown umbrellas and begging bowls and whose canine population is probably the most miserable in the world. The Buddhists will not kill a dog even if it is hopelessly ill or injured. Bangkok nights are made hideous by the howling of these helpless, suffering animals. Its unique silverware—shaped, blackened, and then engraved—is as beautiful today as it ever was. The makers of it form one craft of the East that has neither been mechanized nor lost the high caliber of its artistry.

Physically, of course, Bangkok has changed through the years.

It now has many modern buildings, paved streets, and other so-called "benefits" of civilizations that it did not have in Anna's time. Politically, too, it is now a constitutional monarchy and not the absolute one it was for thousands of years up to 1932. But outside of Bangkok—the one city of any consequence—the Thai countryside is much the same as it has always been.

Rice is the principal food crop and the huge water buffalo the main work animal in the agricultural regions. Back in the teak forests the elephant is the beast of burden. Four-bladed windmills are almost as numerous in the rice fields as they are in Holland. They furnish the horsepower to lift the water out of the small rivers and canals that bisect the alluvial plains around Bangkok and into the irrigation ditches leading to the paddies of rice, which, as in most Asia, is cultivated in flooded fields.

Thailand came out of the war physically and economically in much better shape than most of its neighbors. Although selected targets were hit by United States and British bombs—particularly Bangkok's electrical and water facilities—its countryside was never a battleground either during the Japanese advance or the Japanese retreat.

Thailand's wartime premier, Pibul Songkram, who returned to power by way of a palace revolution in 1947, took Thailand into the war on the side of Japan, but neither he nor the country paid much of a price for that action. Parts of Indo-China and of Malaya, which were given Thailand as part of the bargain with Japan, and to which she did have some historical and ethnic claim, had to be returned. But Thailand did not suffer an onerous occupation by Japan, as did Indo-China, Malaya, and Indonesia. Her land was not fought over as were China, Burma, the Phillipines, and many of the Pacific islands. The Japanese surrender was not followed by civil war. Because of the prestige of her underground leaders and the attitude of her people, peace broke out almost immediately and the Allied occupation was only nominal and relatively inexpensive to her. No belligerent country ever received more generous terms after defeat. This was because she played little part in the war and because it was the American belief that her people had been led unwillingly into the Japanese camp.

When Thailand joined with Japan on December 7, 1941, her minister in Washington, Seni Pramoj, formed what he called the Free Thai Movement. He found ready adherents among leading Siamese both inside and outside Thailand. Most prominent among these were Pridi Phamomyong and Khuang Aphaiwong. Pridi was one of the great prewar leaders of Thailand. It was he who led the 1932 "revolution" that made Thailand a constitutional monarchy. Khuang, a former government official, became the active leader of the resistance movement within the country. His code name for Allied contacts was "Betty." That of Pridi was "Ruth."

Because a base in Thailand would have been of doubtful value to the Allies, until the very last stages of the war, no uprising ever was carried out by the Thai underground, although one was planned for late August of 1945; the Japanese surrender made it unnecessary. Much valuable information was sent out through this underground, however, to Major General William J. Donovan's Office of Strategic Services (the famous OSS) in India. Secret Thai radio stations provided weather data that helped air operations against Burma, Malaya, and Indo-China.

When the Japanese surrendered, the underground, led by Siamese well known to all their countrymen, was ready to move in and set up a government in Bangkok, which was done. Pibul Songkram was arrested. Instead of being tried and hanged, as he probably expected, he was sent instead only into restricted retirement, from which he emerged in November, 1947, to overthrow the government led by some of the men who had treated him so leniently. A shrewd political opportunist, his return brought no break in the good relations between Thailand and the United States. It is one Asiatic country where United States prestige remained high through the immediate postwar years.

Although Thailand declared war on the United States, the United States did not declare war on it. When Britain moved in at the surrender to impose a hard peace, the United States intervened to secure softer terms. In the years since, many United States business firms have entered the country to break the economic hold that Britain had maintained for scores of years on Thailand's foreign trade. It is the one Asiatic country where an American is the chief political adviser to the government. All these factors add up to diplomatic and business relations that are as friendly as those between any two nations in the world.

Economically, Thailand was in a fortunate position at war's end. She was able to produce the one thing that most of the rest of Asia needed—rice. Burma and Indo-China, the other two surplus rice countries of Southeast Asia, both were in a state of civil war. Indonesia never had grown more than enough for her own people, and although the Republican government did make a barter with India to exchange rice for cotton cloth, only small quantities moved through the Dutch blockade.

One of the demands made on Thailand by Britain in the peace terms that were softened through United States intervention was for 1,500,000 tons of rice the first peace year as war indemnity. The eventual solution was purchase of the rice by a Tripartite Committee, of which the United States and Britain were members. Because of the decrease during the war years of Thailand's rice output—from 4,560,000 tons in 1939 to 3,458,000 tons in 1945—the quota was set at 800,000 tons for export, and after several adjustments, a price finally was agreed on that gave the Thai farmer a fair return and also brought out all available surplus stores. At the low price first set, the Thai preferred to eat their rice rather than sell it.

Thailand's other two main products—tin and rubber—also were in great demand when peace came. Britain, through her merchant connections in Bangkok, once had a monopoly on these two exports. Although both eventually found their way to the United States, the tin by way of the Singapore smelters, the Siamese were paid in sterling which they could spend only in Britain, and Britain realized a handsome sum of dollars. James T. Scott, the United States commercial attaché at the Bangkok Legation (now an Embassy) broke both these British monopolies. When the British trading companies refused to sell him rubber at the price he was willing to pay (the United States was buying crude rubber directly to stockpile it), he called in the Chinese merchants who theretofore had not dealt in that material. From them he was able to purchase in 1946 a total of 20,000 tons, which was more than the British companies had guaranteed to deliver. Erection by the United States of its own tin smelter at Texas City, Texas, as a war measure, made it possible to ship the high grade Thai ore—which is 90 per cent pure against the 45 per cent to 50 per cent grading of the Bolivian ores that are America's other chief source of supply—directly to the States, by-passing the Singapore smelters.

A wispy little career diplomat, whose hobby is collecting cigarette holders, Mr. Scott proved a thorn in the side of the old British monopolists in other ways. Until 1946 the British had most of the sea traffic—and not very efficient sea traffic. The British captains said that sand bars in the Menan River, which connects Bangkok with the Gulf of Siam, made it impossible to bring any but small ocean tramps into the Bangkok docks. Shipments had to be taken on lighters to ships anchored in the Gulf of Siam. Jimmy Scott didn't believe the Menan was unnavigable; the Siamese told him differently. Neither did agents of the Isthmian Steamship Company, which was expanding its Asia trade. Secret soundings were made during what were ostensibly fishing trips up and down the Menan. These soundings confirmed that the Menan was navigable for big freighters. In the fall of 1946 the Isthmian Line sent one of its flossiest ships, the *Kelso Victory*, of 10,000 tons displacement, steaming up the Menan to tie up to the Bangkok docks. She was polished like a man o' war. Open house was held aboard the *Kelso Victory* and as many of Bangkok's estimated 1,000,000 inhabitants as could get aboard were shown through the ship. When she sailed a few days later, she had a full passenger list and her holds were laden with Siamese products. The service has been continued.

The same thing happened in negotiations for airport privileges for American firms. The British sought an exclusive contract.

They made the mistake, in their prospectus, however, of calling the Singapore-Bangkok run a "shuttle service." When Pan American Airways sought permission to make Bangkok its Southeast Asia headquarters, they got the contract and the air port facilities.

American mining firms also have sent agents into Thailand in an attempt to discover new tin ore deposits. The present mines are British controlled and the usual methods of prospecting cannot be used in jungle country. The American mining agents do most of their prospecting in Bangkok, studying topography and mineral maps of the country, assaying ores and listening to the various stories that are brought them by the Siamese. Only when map, legend, and rock samples indicate a possible tin deposit is it worth while to equip an expedition and hack a path through the jungle to the scene of the alleged tin.

All of which is not to say that Thailand does not have her problems. The Japanese stripped the country of what they needed, paying in scrip, which was worthless after the surrender. What Thailand needed to rebuild her economy was high priced. The result was an inflation that pressed heavily on small shopkeepers and city workers. The black market quoted the pound sterling and the American dollar at triple the official rate. Inflation never, however, reached the proportions that it did in China. Given a stable government for a few years, Thailand could be the most economically strong country in Asia.

Politically, the picture is not so bright. In the first year after the war, Thailand had four governments. Because public office is a monopoly for the few, the changes were politically not important. What was important was that none of the governments were in power long enough to do anything about making the bureaus more efficient or wiping out the corruption that is almost a way of life in Asia since the war. The Thai's word for it freely translates "lubrication." In order to get the smallest detail attended to, Bangkok residents said, it was necessary to "lubricate" the officials concerned.

It is not surprising that this is so. Civil servants in Asia have never had that high dedication to service that the British have built up through the centuries. During the war years it was patriotic to graft from the Japanese. In fact, it was encouraged by the conquerors, who were old hands at the business. With the peacetime inflation it was almost impossible for a minor official to live unless he could make something on the side. The grafting in Thailand was no worse than elsewhere.

Whatever else Pibul Songkram's return to power meant, it did offer Thailand a stability it had not had under other governments. Premier Songkram's record does not promise much in the way of democracy for Thailand, but all history proves that a people that once has known liberty is restive when it is taken away. Twice during the last two decades Thailand has been a democratically ruled country. It would be against history to say it would not again achieve that estate. Premier Songkram, too, is now so worried by the Communists' victories in China that he has dropped some of his dictatorial airs. It is to his advantage to stay on the good side of the Western democracies, and to do that he knows he must permit at least a semblance of rule by the people.

For everyone except her kings, Thailand has been a fairly stable and happy land in a sea of colonialism, war, and civil war. For kings, conditions have changed since the last century. King Prajadhipok—whose visits to the United States in the twenties for operations on his eyes will be remembered by Americans—resigned in 1932 when the throne was made a constitutional and not an absolute monarchy. He died in exile in Switzerland. His nephew, and successor, the late King Ananda Mahidol, was found dead in his bedchamber on June 9, 1946. Whether he committed suicide, shot himself accidentally with one of the target pistols of which he had many, or whether he was murdered has not been definitely determined and perhaps never will be.

Many stories were told in Bangkok. One that was widely believed, despite its official denial, was that he killed himself for love of a Swiss girl whom his mother had forbade him to marry.

This story was that a farewell note to this girl was found in his hand but that it was destroyed.

Ananda's body lay for years crushed in a golden urn awaiting the ceremonial cremation that could not be carried out until the return of King Phumibol Aduldet, who was studying in Switzerland at the time of his brother's death. The new king showed no inclination to return to a land that had meant only heartbreak and death for his uncle and his brother.

Thailand's thousands of years of history are easier to read than her future. Her 200,000 square miles once were occupied by a homogeneous people. In recent years, however, there has been a steady inflow of Chinese—the influx was at a rate of 20,000 to 30,000 a month in the immediate postwar years. Today there are an estimated 3,000,000 to 4,000,000 Chinese among Thailand's population of 19,000,000 to 20,000,000.

That is not an overwhelming number, as compared to Malaya, where Chinese outnumber the Malays. But the Chinese of Thailand have an even more prominent economic position than do those of Singapore and the Federation. They do not grow rice, but they are the middlemen who market it. They own most of the stores in Bangkok and even have a virtual monopoly of the rickshaw business there (a tri-cycle rickshaw that is called a "samlar") although they have to hire the Thai to ride them, since they are forbidden by laws to operate them themselves.

This Chinese community has the strongest tie with China, as is true of Chinese everywhere. During the civil war in China their loyalties were divided. The richer Chinese were for Chiang Kai-shek. The poorer Chinese—coolies in an alien land—were easy converts to communism. Several bloody battles were fought in the streets of Siam over the issue that had China itself in turmoil.

How the Chinese in Thailand eventually will go politically may determine how all Thailand will go. Being a farmer, the average Thai would seem a poor subject for Communist doctrine. The Chinese Communists, however, are strong in the labor forces of

Bangkok, and are believed to have gained many Thai adherents. If the richer Chinese should decide that they could "do business" with a Communist China, the movement might gain that which it now lacks—funds to arm its members. It is well known what a few well armed men can do among a peacefully inclined people, which is what the Thai are.

Thailand offers a better opportunity for a stand against communism than almost any other country of Southeast Asia, if the West is able to demand that Premier Songkram play according to democratic rules and if it is willing to cooperate in seeing that Thailand's economy remains stable and her people prosperous.

PART IX. THE UNITED STATES' COLONIAL PROBLEM

CHAPTER 1. *America's Pacific Colonies*

From the hilltop above the battered old town of Agana, the capital of Guam, is one of the finest views in the Pacific. North and south lie the thirty wooded miles of the island. To westward is Apra Harbor, with a protected anchorage big enough to take a fleet of one hundred ships or more. To the northward and eastward are great airfields on which the world's largest planes can land.

Inhabiting Guam are 25,000 of the Pacific's finest peoples, predominately Malayan, with a strain of Polynesian, and 60,000 to 70,000 United States Navy, Army, Air Force, and Marine personnel, uniformed and civilian. The latter make Guam the United States' best equipped, largest manned Pacific island base. It is also the center of Navy trusteeship activities in the Pacific, the trusteed island groups of the Carolines, Marshalls, and the rest of the Marianne chain, which were taken from Japan in the Pacific War in 1941–1945, being governed from there. It is a very important place for the United States.

Guam was ceded to the United States in the Treaty of Paris of 1898 that ended the Spanish-American War. It had been taken from the Spanish without a fight during the war. Article IX of the Treaty provided that "the civil rights and political status of the native inhabitants of the territories hereby ceded to the United States shall be determined by Congress." As this is written (late 1949), over fifty years later, Congress has not yet gotten around to doing anything. The Guamanians, now outnumbered on their own islands, are still "nationals" of the United States, not citizens. It was not until 1937 that a bill was introduced to make them citizens. It was not until 1946 that an Organic Act was introduced in Congress to give them by law the protection of the Bill of Rights and the other rights of citizenship to which they have long since proved themselves entitled.

The Guamanians have not been badly treated. The health record of the island is good. They are an advanced people, socially, intellectually, and economically, as Pacific peoples go. The shame is that for over fifty years, because of the neglect of Congress, they have been treated as second-class citizens, ruled by men and not under law, in negation of the principles on which was founded the United States of America.

Until September 3, 1949, when President Truman, by Executive Order 10,077, appointed Carlton Skinner, of the Department of the Interior, Governor of Guam, the island people had been under the rule of the Navy Department, whose first concern was military, and not the welfare of the people. No matter how good such a government is, it is a rule of men. The law on Guam was what the Navy office in charge said it was. One made it an offense for a Guamanian to sing or whistle after a certain hour within two blocks of the governor's residence; his wife's sleep had been disturbed by some happy Guamanians. Captain Bradley, the Navy governor in 1930, promulgated a Bill of Rights for the Guamanians, but any succeeding governor could have abrogated it.

Because their numbers were small and their voices weak, the Guamanians were the forgotten people of the "colonial empire" of the United States until the Japanese attack in December, 1941, focused attention on them. When the islands were liberated in June and July, 1944, it was learned that they had behaved heroically under Japanese occupation. For three years they had not only refused to cooperate with the Japanese, they had successfully hidden on their small island a survivor of the Navy garrison that had been stationed there. Many of them died under torture, refusing to reveal his whereabouts. For their shabby treatment they had returned as fine a loyalty as any people living under the American flag.

While the war continued, their island was built into the major United States base in the Pacific, headquarters of the Pacific Fleet, thus subjecting it to continued Japanese attack. Since the Japanese capitulated, more of their land has been taken away for military installations, their claims for war damage were poorly handled, and Congress continued to postpone the granting to them of the rights and privileges to which they surely were entitled on the record. Even their best beaches were taken from them for use as military recreation areas, and put out of bounds to them.

For the foreseeable future, Guam will be a major United States military base, with military personnel outnumbering the Guamanians by three to one, or more. Which is all the more reason why the Guamanians should be made citizens, why they should have their own civil government to treat for them as equals with the military and to protect them against undue encroachment. No matter what the cost (and it could not possibly be very large) their cities, which were largely destroyed by United States shells and bombs in the retaking of the island, should be rebuilt. They should be protected by law against further seizure of their land or denial of their civil rights, no matter what military necessity is pleaded. The duty of making their own laws and of governing themselves should be granted them by act of Congress just as soon as possible.

Guam is on the direct air routes from the United States to Asia. It is, in effect, a show window. It is a sorry spectacle the United States has on display there now, no matter how shiny the surface, for the leaders of Asia to look at when they pass through. It is a spectacle of a people treated as wards, and not as equals. If the people of the United States believe, as they say they do, that it is right that makes might, and not vice versa, then they should demand from Congress action to right this ancient wrong that has been done to the Guamanians merely because they were too weak for their voices to be heard in Washington.

The other important prewar Pacific possession of the United States where conditions similar to those on Guam prevail is American Samoa, which also has been under Navy governance since its acquisition in 1898 by the United States in a deal with Great Britain and Germany. Unlike Guam, Samoa has little military significance. It was never more than a minor United States naval base, even during the war with Japan. Its people number only about 18,000, and they are not as well educated nor as Americanized as are the Guamanians. There is no less reason, though, why the Samoans should not either be made citizens or be freed entirely. The former status is preferred, because they need American protection, economically, today as much as they ever have.

The Samoans, who are unmixed Polynesian, have retained the old tribal structure of pre-Western days. They have their Council of Chiefs, or Fono, to advise the Navy governor on matters affecting them. The pattern of their life has remained that of the old days, of separate villages run on a communal basis. Its economy is largely agricultural, not military as is Guam.

Every official and unofficial commission visiting the islands has found the Samoans fully qualified for United States citizenship, and entitled to it. Until such time as there is an island grouping, and complete independence from Western powers of all the South Pacific islands, they will need the help and protection of the United States. Since their islands offered the United States for over fifty years a Navy fueling and signal-relay station that it thought it needed, such financial help until the island peoples are ready to run their own affairs again should not be too high a price to pay.

The other Pacific islands over which flew the American flag in pre-Pearl Harbor days—Wake, Midway, Canton, and Enderbury (the latter two shared with Britain)—were uninhabited when occupied as air stations, and offer no such problem as do Guam, Samoa, and the trusteed islands. They can be kept, or they can be abandoned, as circumstances dictate, without any violation of human rights. None of them is self-sustaining.

What is to happen to the Marianas, the Carolines, and the Marshalls—now held under trusteeship by the United States—is for decision in some distant tomorrow. The estimated 85,000 people who inhabit those islands are now, however, wards of the United

States, and greater efforts should be made than were made in the first few years of trusteeship to help them advance toward self-government. These islands were the happy hunting grounds of the early explorers and exploiters. Under the Germans, and then the Japanese after 1917, their inhabitants were held as slaves, without rights or duties. Many of them were battlegrounds, and nearly all suffered in some degree or other from the war.

Although the Navy has not treated them since the war as did the Germans and the Japanese, the record of accomplishment is not impressive. Few of the islands have resources above mere subsistence. Two of them—Bikini and Eniwetok—have been used as testing grounds for atom bombs. The record of the handling of the people taken off both has been disgraceful. Consent was sought from both peoples, ostensibly, but no choice really was given; and they have been unhappy, according to reports, on their new island homes.

That the Navy has been conscious of its shortcomings is recorded in the fact that they have allowed few correspondents to go into the area since the war, and no one who they suspected would turn in a poor report. What really has been happening there under United States trusteeship thus remains a mystery.

Like Guam and Samoa, the ultimate solution must be as much self-government as is possible, and the placing of the island people under civil administration, governing under a code of law.

What the United States needs now, and has needed for many years, is some Government division, or a new department, to administer its offshore possessions, which include Puerto Rico and the Virgin Islands in the Caribbean, as well as Guam, Samoa, and the trusteed islands of the Pacific.

Establishment of such an office was on the agenda of President Roosevelt when he took office in 1934. He did set up, in the Department of the Interior, the Division of Territories and Island Possessions, and appointed the able Ernest Gruening, later Governor of Alaska, as its first head. Mr. Gruening held the job for seven years, but there have been five directors since he left, none approaching his competence. Guam and Samoa remained, of course, under the Navy.

The Department of the Interior hardly seems the place for such an important division, however, any more than does the Navy Department or the new Department of National Defense. What seems indicated is establishment of a new Department of Overseas Territories to carry out the responsibilities of the United States in the outlying islands. It should be manned by experts—expert geologists, ecologists, anthropologists, botanists, zoologists, in addition to expert administrators.

The United States can do no less than to present to the world a model government for weak and scattered peoples, and a model trusteeship under the United Nations.

Hawaii and Alaska

The only two organized Territories of the United States were, in late 1949, well on the road toward incorporation as the forty-ninth and fiftieth states of the Union. Both had been petitioning for such action for several years.

Alaska, purchased from Russia in 1867 for $7,200,000, and the Hawaiian Islands, which acceded to the United States in 1898, both were colonized by mainlanders, who now outnumber the former inhabitants of both places. The 1939 census showed 40,000 whites against 32,000 Indians and Aleuts in Alaska. The division in Hawaii, according to the 1948 census, is 180,480 whites and only 80,760 Hawaiians among the Islands' population of 540,500. The other racial groups are divided as follows: 176,280 Japanese (most of them born in the Islands of parents brought there as contract laborers forty to fifty years ago), 53,640 Filipinos, 30,530 Chinese, 9,820 Puerto Ricans, 7,320 Koreans, and 1,670 of other national origins, mostly Asiatic. They make of Hawaii, where no racial discrimination is tolerated legally, the melting pot of the Pacific.

Both Alaska and Hawaii are important economically and militarily to the United States. The former, especially, has had its riches only partially explored and exploited. As knowledge of how to live in cold climates, and the ability to do so, increases, it should become even more important economically. Both are important fueling stops en route to and from the United States and Asia by air.

Hawaii and Alaska have a long record of stable and enlightened Territorial government, especially Hawaii, and have been well qualified for years for statehood. The old argument against statehood, that they were noncontiguous territories, still infected some congressional minds, but it was not taken as a serious argument, since both have been for years within a few hours' flight of Stateside bases. The war also provided a definitive answer to the question of the loyalty of the Japanese in the Hawaiian Islands.

Like establishment of civil government and considerable self-government in Guam and Samoa, admittance to the Union of Hawaii and Alaska should have an important psychological effect in Asia. Action on both counts would show the East that there was at least one Western country which lived up to its stated principles.

PART X. THE FUTURE OF ASIA

What the world calls Western civilization had its birth, and it has its center today, on the shores of two bodies of water—the Mediterranean Sea and the North Atlantic Ocean. First came the Mediterranean, on whose shores rose the early empires of written history. Then the balance shifted to the north and west, to the countries bordering on the North Atlantic. Today its center is Washington. Intriguing and important questions for Europe and the Americas are: Will the westward trend continue? Will the lands fronting on the Pacific basin be the dominant ones in tomorrow's world?

On the eastward side of the Pacific is the world's greatest industrial country, the United States. On its westward shores live one-half the world's people. A marriage of the two Pacific basin areas, a union of the technology of the United States with the abundant man power of the Pacific countries (in which India should be included because her destiny is linked with Asia, not with Europe) could create a new world. It could even create a new civilization, an amalgam of East and West which would take from each that which is best.

It is a question that must be answered soon, or one on which a start must be made toward the answer, on a much broader scale than that envisioned in Point Four of President Truman's 1948 Inaugural Address—that is, if Asia is to develop along democratic lines instead of as a group of powerful Communistic states attached to Moscow.

Soviet Russia is not now in a position to give the Chinese Communists or other Asiatic governments the technological assistance and the machines that are needed to transform Asia from an agricultural to an industrial economy. But she may have them in ten or fifteen years. The West—which means primarily the United States—has that long, perhaps, in which to convince Asia's millions that our way of life is preferable to that practiced in the USSR.

There are several circumstances that favor the West in a contest for the allegiance of the East in addition to the head start it has in industrial power. The most important is that the Asiatic is more individualistic than is the Westerner. Life there has always been, and it is today, based on the family and the individual, and not on the State. It is true even of Japan. The emperor is not the State, although the militarists set him up as a symbol of it and used him for their own purposes. To the average Japanese he is the Father, the head of the family. The Zaibatsu, the Japanese trusts, were family trusts, primarily.

What is true of Japan is doubly so of China. Dr. Sun Yat-sen, the father of the Chinese Revolution, first embraced and then renounced communism as the political framework for a united China. He became convinced that it was not the solution for his country and his people. Mao Tse-tung and the other leaders of the Communist revolution quote Dr. Sun more often than they do Marx, Lenin, or Stalin in discussing their plans and laying down their program for China. They stress the dignity and the responsibility of the individual, not that of an amorphous State. It is the Chinese peasant to whom they make their appeal, not to a faceless proletariat.

The real leaders of the nationalist movements in Indo-China, in Indonesia, in Malaya, in Burma, are not Marxists. They are nationalists. Ho Chi Minh, the Indo-Chinese leader, says: "Once I was a Communist. Now I am a Viet Namese." Those nationalist leaders who have turned to communism, such as Sjariffoedin in Indonesia, have done so more in despair than because of an ideological conviction. There is not a first-class intellect among the present Communist leaders in Asia, if the thesis is accepted that the

Chinese leaders are more nationalists than Marxists, which most people do accept who have had contact with them or who have studied their writings and their programs.

Convincing Asia that democracy is preferable to the police state communism has always imposed is not as large a task as it may seem. Asia has one billion people, but only a small educated minority. Convince the leaders of Asia that democracy is the better way and then help them to institute democratic programs the emphasis of which is on the education and the betterment of the individual, and the job is done.

Which is not to say that winning Asia's leaders to the side of the West will be an easy effort. The white man, en masse, does not have a good reputation in the Far East. There is the record of colonialism in India, Burma, Malaya, Indonesia, and Indo-China to be overcome. There is the record of the treaty ports and of extraterritoriality in China to be wiped off the slate with a clean cloth. There is the record of the West's support of corrupt, inefficient regimes, such as that of Chiang Kai-shek in China, to be nullified by good deeds. There is the record of the abandonment of Korea to the not so gentle mercies of the Japanese in the period from 1905 to 1945 that will not be easily forgotten or forgiven, and the exploitation of Manchuria by the same Japanese in the twenties and the thirties, about which the West did nothing but talk.

They are not fools, these Asiatic leaders. They can have few illusions about Soviet Russia. But if they have only the choice of Moscow or the old order, they will turn to the Kremlin in the belief that domination by the USSR could be no worse than that they have known for the last three hundred years, and that it might be better. Just to point to the Soviet record in Eastern Europe is not enough to dissuade them from that hope.

The day when nationalism in Asia could be contained by force of arms, such as it was in India by the British in other days, in their colonies by the French and the Dutch, in China by Western forces during the Taiping and Boxer rebellions, has long since passed.

Temporary victories by those means might still be won. But they would settle nothing.

Even more so than in Europe, the approach in Asia must be a positive one. The first step, and the most difficult one, is understanding. The East is different from the West. It is different in way of life, it is different in its religions, it is different in its attitudes. But not as different as many think.

It is difficult for a Westerner to understand the communal rioting in India, the callousness with which the East passes by the man starving in the street. But are we so different? Is the brutality of the Germans toward the Jews and the peoples of the countries of Europe they conquered understandable to us because the Germans had white skins, while the communal rioting in India is not, because the atrocities there were done by men with a different pigmentation?

It is wrong to assume that the Asiatic does not feel pain and hunger and despair, and that he does not cherish hope for better things tomorrow. If the white man is inclined to turn his back on Asia in the belief that understanding is beyond his abilities, he should reread the saying of Terence the African, the black slave of Rome, who wrote several hundred years ago: "I am a man; nothing human is alien to me." If there is that basic approach, the problems of Asia assume more understandable proportions.

There are two fallacies about Asia that seem endemic among most Americans and some Europeans. One is that Asia had her day a long time ago, that the Far East is now a stagnant area of the world, with depleted resources about which nothing can be done and which has no future. The second is that the problems of Asia are somehow separate from those of the United States and the rest of the West.

As to the first fallacy, there have been other civilizations which rose and fell and then rose again. There is no reason why Asia cannot recover from her hundreds of years of lethargy. What has happened in China since Dr. Sun first lighted the torch of revolution in Canton in 1912 is sufficient answer to the first. Had the West supported that revolution in its early phases, the Japanese might not have dared to attack China and attempt her dismemberment.

Asia's known natural resources have been depleted. Her forests have been cut, her land farmed out to such an extent that its insufficient fertility now is maintained in China only by the use of excrement from the bodies of its inhabitants, which is a losing proposition. But Asia's rivers, if controlled, could provide the electricity to run the nitrogen plants to extract from the air enough fertilizer, it is estimated, to increase the productivity of her soil by at least 25 per cent. Forests can be replanted. Her mineral resources have never been even properly surveyed. Who knows what riches may be hidden in some of her mountain ranges? A free India has many projects under way, and others planned, which will eventually irrigate much of her waste land and restore fertility to depleted soils. Indonesians estimate that only a fraction of the mineral wealth of their country has been tapped.

The second fallacy, that Asia is a problem separate from that of Europe, is one held largely by Americans. The Dutch know how closely the fortunes of their small country are bound to those of the East Indies. The French, groaning at the large part of the defense budget spent since 1945 on fighting a losing war in Indo-China, know that what happens there, and in Africa, is vitally important to metropolitan France. The British, guarding Hong Kong, acting as banker for India, Australia, New Zealand, Malaya, and other smaller areas, know how much of their old way of life depended on exploitation of the riches of the East. One of the most important British ministerial posts is the Colonial Office, and one of the most important boards is that which is entrusted with Colonial development. It will be useless to contain communism in Europe and let Asia go to Russia by default. They are indivisible parts of one world.

If Asia is to be saved for democracy, these policies would seem to be indicated, country by country:

India—As full aid as possible through loans, machinery, and technical assistance to harness her rivers, to irrigate and replenish her soil, to survey her resources and to aid in their development.

China—Recognition of the Communist Government at Peiping as ruler of most of China, and the driving of as hard and as fair a bargain as is possible for what the West has to give and which China desperately needs in return for guarantees of fundamental human rights to the Chinese themselves.

Indo-China—Guarded, non-military help to the Bao Dai Government if, as and when it appears it will have the support of a majority of the people and will not be merely a puppet of France. This help should be of a character that will benefit the people directly and advance their health and their education.

Indonesia—As with India, the extension to the new United States of Indonesia of as much aid as is needed, and can be conveniently used, to make again available to the world the riches of raw materials that are there in such abundance.

Malaya—As rapid a progression as the Malayans themselves want toward self-government and independence, along with assistance to survey and exploit (for the benefit of the people of Malaya themselves) the peninsula's untapped resources.

Siam—Guarded aid made contingent on fully democratic government, with elections decided by ballot instead of by bullet.

Pacific Island Groups—A careful watch within the United Nations on the trustee powers and on the South Pacific Commission to see that the rights of the Island peoples are fully protected and their welfare placed above security or any other considerations.

Asia is half of one world. Our world. The only one we have. The shape of things to come is there, as well as in Europe. The first half of the twentieth century saw more changes in the face of the world than all of the nineteenth century did. The second half could be even more revolutionary. The first ten years of that second fifty could be the decisive ones. What will the answer be?

INDEX

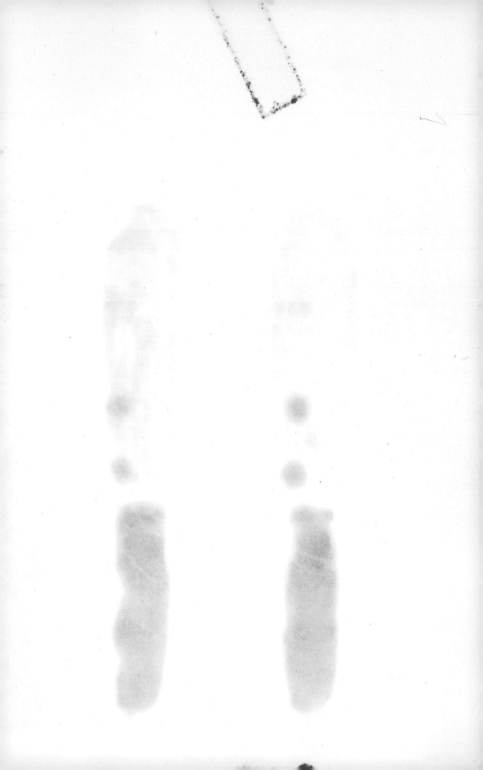

Al [illegible]
M [illegible]

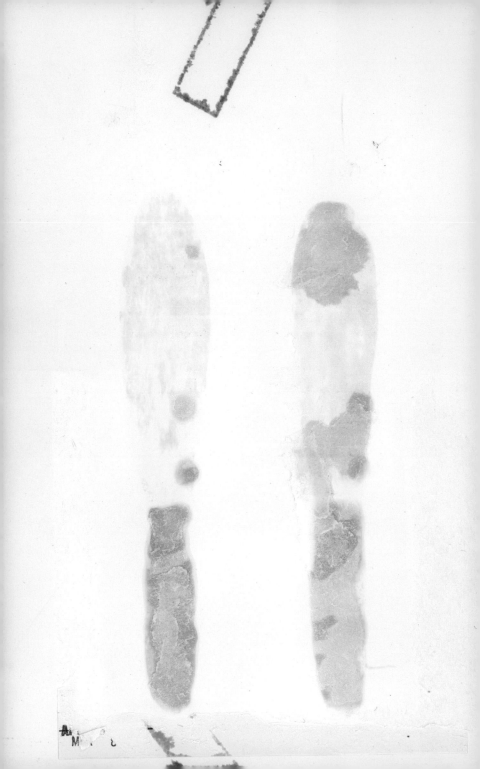